stress relief

TO GO

stress relief
TO GO

Jonathan Hilton

An Hachette Livre UK Company

First published in Great Britain in 2008 by
Gaia Books, a division of Octopus Publishing Group Ltd
2–4 Heron Quays, London E14 4JP
www.octopusbooks.co.uk

Copyright © Octopus Publishing Group Ltd 2008

Distributed in the United States and Canada by
Sterling Publishing Co., Inc.
387 Park Avenue South, New York, NY 10016-8810

This material was previously published as *A Gaia Busy Person's Guide: Stress Relief*

ISBN: 978-185675-300-5

A CIP catalogue record for this book is available from the British Library

Printed and bound in China

10 9 8 7 6 5 4 3 2 1

Cautionary note:
All reasonable care has been taken in the preparation of this book, but the information it contains is not meant to take the place of medical care under the direct supervision of a doctor. Before making any changes in your health regime, always consult a doctor. While all the therapies detailed in this book are completely safe if done correctly, you must seek professional advice if you are in any doubt about any medical condition. Any application of the ideas and information contained in this book is at the reader's sole discretion and risk.

Direction Patrick Nugent
Production Simone Nauerth
Editors Jonathan Hilton, Jo Godfrey Wood
Design Peggy Sadler
Principal Photography Ruth Jenkinson
Photography Martin Norris
Proofreading and Index Kathie Gill

Contents

Introduction

Stress is a difficult concept to get a proper handle on. Suggest to some people that stress may be a problem and you are met with derision. "What's wrong with a bit of stress? I wouldn't get up in the morning if it weren't for the stress in my life. It keeps me going. Don't know what the fuss is all about." To other people, however, stress is something that dominates their entire lives – a dark, formless, frightening beast stalking their waking and sleeping hours. But before looking at why people can have such different reactions, often, essentially, to the same set of circumstances, it is necessary to think about what stress actually is.

The difficulty we have in defining stress is that it is not a single medical condition. Nor does it conform to a set of common medical symptoms. Rather, stress is a combination of problems – mental, physical, and emotional, and the symptoms people experience are by no means straightforward either. These can include generalized feelings of ill-health, headaches, migraines, and postural problems; taking in conditions such as fatigue, heart palpitations, weight fluctuations, irritability, digestive ailments, and outbursts of inappropriate anger or aggression; as well as muscular disorders, sexual dysfunction, skin problems, mood swings, and full-blown depression.

Of course, nobody ever exhibits all these disturbing symptoms at once; rather, a person's reaction to stress expresses itself through the body's weakest physiological system. But the resulting specific illness or set of illnesses may be just the tip of an iceberg.

MASSAGE
Many forms of massage are perfect for relieving the types of tension headache and migraine that are commonly associated with stress.

In essence, stress is the body's response to changes and the pressure that can place on us – changes in the environment (noise levels, living conditions, constant traffic jams, moving house); changes at work (personal conflict with a colleague, promotion, demotion, redundancy); changes in personal circumstances (getting married/divorced, going on vacation, money worries). But, depending on the complexities of an individual's personality, upbringing, and life experiences, what one person perceives as an intolerable strain can be regarded by another as a pulse-raising, though thoroughly enjoyable, challenge.

Indeed, it is true to say that without the motivation that stress brings about we would all find it pretty difficult to make enough effort to achieve even the most modest of goals. Stress usually becomes a problem only when the changes being experienced

escalate and, with no time to adjust and compensate for the changing landscape, we find ourselves in a constant and prolonged state of stress arousal.

This state of arousal is commonly referred to as the "fight-or-flight" response. It is a primitive reaction to danger or threat that has been carried forward to the modern world from the time when personal survival meant, literally, fighting an adversary or fleeing from, say, a marauding wild animal.

This response, with the complex series of physiological adaptations it imposes on the body, is often inappropriate in today's world, where life-threatening danger rarely looms around every corner. Nevertheless, our bodies still respond as they have always done, and a prolonged state of arousal – even at a relatively low level – can fatigue and weaken our system, impair the functioning of our body's immune system, and eventually bring about a malfunction or illness.

ABOUT THIS BOOK

Many of the problems, both psychological and physiological, resulting from the anxiety and tension of prolonged periods of stress can be successfully managed. More than that, you can even learn to turn stressful situations to your own advantage. The key to this is, first, to recognize the situations that cause you the distress – the factors (known as stressors) that trigger the stress response – and then, second, to intervene, using the most appropriate of the various therapies detailed in this book, to short-circuit your body's normal destructive response. The key therapies dealt with in the book include aromatherapy, chi kung, colour and crystal healing, feng shui, massage,

RELATIONSHIPS
A relaxed and open relationship, with good lines of communication between you and your partner, can be one of the best antidotes to stress (opposite).

meditation, neuro-linguistic programming, pilates, reflexology, reiki, and yoga. By learning to achieve a balance between tension and relaxation, when to fight your corner and when to go with the flow, you can rapidly bring about a positive change in every aspect of your professional and personal life.

The first chapter of this book looks at what stress is, what the common stressors are, how stress and personality interact, and sets out the basic principles of how, with a heightened understanding of your adversary, you can start to alter your stress responses.

The next three chapters take you though a "typical" day, explaining how, from first thing in the morning, before you even get out of bed, you can start stress-proofing your life. Throughout the book, the different therapies are explained and illustrated, showing you how, for instance, to cope with the strains and stresses of the daily grind to work – whether by car, public transport, or flying off somewhere on a business trip. And for many of us, it's only when we get to work that the stress really kicks in. Many examples of work-day situations are covered in this chapter, and the solutions to the problems illustrated can easily be adapted to suit your particular circumstances.

In the final chapter, the bedrock that is family life and friendship is emphasized. The nature of stress is that it infiltrates every aspect of your life and care must be taken that the ones you need most are not the ones put most at risk.

EXERCISE
Working on two levels, exercise helps to counter the adverse effects of stress. First, it acts as a distraction, taking your mind off your problems. Second, it burns off the stress-inducing hormones in the bloodstream produced by the body when you feel under pressure or threatened.

CHAPTER ONE

A stressful life?

Stress reactions to the typically high-pressured lives
we lead today are largely hardwired into our brains.
These reactions are an evolutionary response to
danger and change, although today these dangers
are more often perceived than real. Change the
perception, and you are halfway there.

A bear comes steadily down the path toward you, its eyes locked on yours. With only the most rudimentary weapons to defend your family, your body's stress responses kick in. You have two choices – run or fight. Either way, your skeletal muscles become engorged with oxygenated blood to increase their strength and stamina, your liver starts converting cortisol into sugar to provide extra energy, stress hormones surge around your body, your eyesight becomes sharper, and your digestion shuts down as all available blood is diverted to the brain.

And these are just the highlights. Our bodies undergo huge adaptations to cope with perceived danger and even though today this danger is more likely to comprise a missed essay deadline, an unsuccessful meeting, an emotional upset or some financial set-back, our bodies still react as if that bear were walking down the path toward us.

Just how well or badly you adapt and respond to stress depends on many factors. What type of personality you have is, for example, crucial, as is the frequency with which you have had to confront change and pressure in the last few months. Your living conditions and the state of your personal and working life are also important factors. Even your general diet has a profound effect on the body's stress responses, as does your participation in some form of regular exercise or sport.

The good news is that all of these factors are within your power to change or modify.

Fight or flight

Pressure, which, for most of us, is part of our lives most of the time, is the force that motivates us to meet life's challenges, to develop and to grow as people, to achieve and to create. Pressure is perceived as stress only when it is experienced at extreme levels or for prolonged periods – though the level at which pressure becomes "problem" stress varies from person to person.

HOW THE BODY RESPONDS

Far back in our ancestral past, when pressures truly were a matter of life and death, the body's response to elevated levels of stress was a series of physical and biochemical changes designed to prepare the individual either to fight or to flee the scene. Popularly known as the "fight-or-flight" response, the changes in the body include the secretion of stress chemicals such as adrenaline and noradrenaline, elevated blood pressure, increased heart rate, increased blood flow to the muscles, and glycogen in the liver converted to blood sugar to provide extra energy. Other arousal responses by the body include a shutdown of the digestive system, which goes some way to explaining the link between stress and ulcers.

OUR EVOLUTIONARY INHERITANCE

The problem of our evolutionary inheritance for us today is that the fight-or-flight response makes no distinction between, say, an approaching essay deadline and a real and immediate physical threat. And without the vigorous exertion involved in either

AROUSAL RESPONSES
When the body is aroused by the fight-or-flight response, a series of changes occur:

- *Lungs – breathing becomes shallow and rapid.*

- *Liver – cortisol converts glycogen into blood sugar.*

- *Adrenal glands – stress chemicals are secreted into the bloodstream.*

- *Cardiovascular – heart rate and blood pressure both increase.*

- *Digestive system – digestion shuts down as blood is diverted from the stomach to the brain and skeletal muscles.*

- *Skin – sweating increases to aid cooling of the body.*

- *Eyes – pupils dilate to sharpen the field of vision.*

fighting or fleeing to use up and neutralize the effects
of the stress hormones surging around the bloodstream,
you are soon likely to feel jittery and tense and even
notice a slight trembling of the hands.

Repeated stress-inducing episodes or prolonged
periods of intense stress cause a range of other
changes in the body, one of the most significant being
the suppression of the immune system, making the
body susceptible to illness and disease.

Stress and personality

There seems to be good evidence that a link exists between the type of personality you have and how susceptible you are to the effects of stress. This is not really surprising, since your personality – the type of person you are – has an enormous influence on how you react to every situation you encounter in life.

PERSONALITY TYPES

The two broad personality types identified – Type A and Type B – determine whether or not you respond to the everyday pressure of life in a stressed or non-stressed fashion. Don't assume, however, that destructive reaction patterns are fixed or immutable.

Type A personalities are those most at risk from the damaging effects of stress. These people are highly motivated, fixated on competing and winning, impatient, hardworking, aggressive, and ambitious. They are the go-getters, the strivers, those driven to push themselves to the point of exhaustion and then, too often, beyond. Their lifestyle is one of near-constant physical arousal.

By way of a contrast, Type B personality types are far more sanguine, relaxed, self-confident, and generally more at ease with themselves. Although not as obviously ambitious as their A counterparts, Type Bs are as likely to do the best possible job they can and achieve the same high standards, though without the trappings of anxiety, panic, and aggression.

It is rare to find that a person fits solely into one or other of these types; it is more usual to discover that personality is a mixture of A and B characteristics.

WARNING SIGNS
Think about modifying your behaviour (see opposite) if you see something of yourself in most of the following:

- *Believe that if you want something done properly, you must do it yourself.*

- *Go to extreme measures to ensure punctuality.*

- *Impatiently finish people's sentences for them.*

- *Feel the need to see more clients, sell more goods, or produce more units than your colleagues.*

- *Become angry if you lose at sport or games.*

- *Find it difficult to sit still and do nothing.*

- *Feel that there are never enough hours in the day to fulfil your responsibilities.*

- *Speak more loudly or quickly than your companions and tend to swear inappropriately.*

MODIFYING YOUR BEHAVIOUR

Once you have recognized the destructive elements of your personality you can set about making changes. Try the following:

- *Think seriously about whether it is better to live to work or to work to live.*

- *Build into your schedule some time each day that is just for you to do precisely what you want.*

- *Accept that you cannot control everything and that things go wrong sometimes.*

- *Resolve to take a lunch break every day away from your desk or workstation.*

- *Listen to other people and resist the temptation to finish other people's sentences for them.*

- *Don't keep looking for fault in others.*

- *Practise relaxation techniques and controlled breathing.*

- *Participate in regular, non-competitive forms of exercise and sport.*

Life events

It is not possible to draw up a list of stressful life situations and events that you could carry around and consult whenever you wanted to reduce your exposure to harm. This is so simply because practically anything you are exposed to through your normal, everyday routine can potentially be stressful at some stage in your life. Supporting this unlikely sounding proposition is this table of life events (see below), which was drawn up in the late 1960s by two American psychologists, T H Holmes and R H Rahe.

The table lists and ranks, in terms of their stress-inducing reactions, a wide range of ordinary life events, covering both your social and working life. Some are obvious stressors, such as the death of your

STRESS-INDUCING EVENT	STRESS RATING	STRESS-INDUCING EVENT	STRESS RATING	
Death of partner	100	Illness of close family member	44	
Break-up of relationship	73	Becoming pregnant	40	
Separation from partner	65	Problems with sex life	39	
Going to prison	63	New family member	39	
Death of close family member	63	Change of job	39	
Injury or serious illness	53	Change in financial state	38	
Marriage	50	Arguments with partner	35	
Losing your job	47	Large mortgage	32	
Getting back with partner	45	Mortgage or loan called in	30	
Retirement	45	Promotion at work	29	

partner, taking out a large mortgage, or losing your job; others, however, are more surprising, such as going on vacation, celebrating Christmas, or winning a promotion at work. What the research made clear was that susceptibility to stress-inducing situations was made worse when changes, positive as well as negative, occurred in clusters, leaving little time in between for you to adapt.

The value of this list is that it acts as a warning. If you are experiencing a period of rapid change in your social and/or professional life, it may be wise to slow things down, taking whatever time *you* require to manage the process safely, ensuring that the seeds of future health problems do not find fertile ground.

HOW DO YOU RATE?

No scale (such as the one reproduced here) can indicate how you would respond to stressful situations, since reactions vary from person to person. However, if you score more than 300 points in a single year it is an indicator that your stress load is high and you may be at increased risk from stress-related illness. Keeping your score below 150 indicates that you are low-risk in terms of stress-related problems.

STRESS-INDUCING EVENT	STRESS RATING	STRESS-INDUCING EVENT	STRESS RATING
Child leaving home	29	Changing school	20
Disputes with in-laws	29	Change in leisure activity	19
Noteworthy achievement	28	Change in religious activity	19
Partner starts/stops working	26	Change in social activity	18
Begins/ends school	26	Small mortgage	17
Change in living		Change in sleeping habits	16
circumstances	25	More/fewer family visits	15
Change in personal habits	24	Change in eating habits	15
Disputes with boss at work	23	Going on vacation	13
Change in hours worked	20	Christmas	12
Moving home	20	Minor breach of law	11

Common stress factors

Look through the lists below, and those on the following pages, to see how many questions you can answer "Yes" to. These are the factors adding to your stress load.

PERSONAL FACTORS
- Do your bad points outnumber your good ones?
- Are you tearful a lot of the time for no obvious reason?
- Do you often fret about what the future holds?
- Do you often find your hands tightly balled into fists?
- Is it difficult to speak to new people?
- Do you regret not having a close friend with whom you can talk through your problems and fears?
- Does worry about the day's events regularly prevent you from getting a good, restful sleep?
- In a group, do you find it difficult to express your opinion?
- Do you feel at ease in your own company?

RELATIONSHIP FACTORS
- Is there insufficient privacy at home?
- Do you often feel disappointed in or embarrassed by your partner's behaviour?
- Are your feelings largely disregarded by your partner?
- Are you failing your family in material terms?
- Are money worries dominating family life?
- Do you want sex more often than your partner?
- Do you often fail to sexually satisfy your partner?
- Are family disputes common and do you often go to bed with bad feelings still unresolved?

ALCOHOL INTAKE
Watch your alcohol intake. Drinking more than the recommended units of alcohol will probably send you off to sleep, though you are likely to wake up again a few hours later. The disruptive effects of alcohol on your system is compounded if you additionally have caffeine-containing drinks, which also stimulate the nervous system and induce anxiety.

COFFEE AND TEA

Doing too many things at once? Feeling stressed and anxious after a punishing day at work, a bad day made worse because you failed to achieve anything like your best performance? Just a few minutes more now sorting out your workload for tomorrow and you can call it a day, sit back and have that cup of coffee you have been promising yourself.

Whether it's coffee, tea, chocolate, cola, or cocoa does not really matter – when your nerves are stretched tight, the caffeine in all of these popular drinks is the last thing you should have (see pp. 24–31).

The energy surge and increased alertness felt after taking caffeine is due to the glycogen in your body being converted into glucose. However, any positive effects you feel will be short-lived as your body's store of glycogen soon runs dry. The tiredness that follows cannot always be corrected by sleep, as the caffeine has stimulated your nervous system and increased the levels of adrenaline circulating in your bloodstream.

WORK FACTORS

- Do you have a difficult relationship with those around you at work?
- Do you work harder than your colleagues?
- Are you bored with the work you do?
- Do you invariably take work home with you in the evenings or work through your lunch break?
- Are you constantly trying to meet tight deadlines?
- Is it difficult to make the time necessary to take your full vacation entitlement each year?
- Is your working environment constantly noisy?
- Are you struggling with new responsibilities having recently been promoted or changed jobs?
- Are lines of communication poor or the chain of responsibility ill-defined?
- Do you feel frustrated because your abilities are not properly appreciated or rewarded?
- Is your work physically demanding all the time?

ENVIRONMENTAL FACTORS

- Do you spend long periods stuck in traffic jams, either as a car driver or on public transport?
- Is your home too small or uncomfortable, or is your immediate neighbourhood dirty and dangerous?
- Is lack of privacy at home an issue?
- Does your mood suffer with the reduced light levels common in the winter months?
- Are you constantly disturbed by traffic or aircraft noise, or does noise from neighbours often intrude?
- Is it difficult for you to get to local parks or other green spaces?
- Is it hard to buy a good range of fresh fruit and vegetables in your local stores?

THE IMPACT OF NOISE

One of the most damaging of all the environmental stress triggers is noise. This is a particular problem in our towns and cities, where background levels of noise can be all-pervasive. But even in more rural environments, don't discount disturbances from a neighbouring avid home handyperson or your teenage children's addiction to loud music.

Even if you block the noise from your conscious mind, your body still produces a stress response. Constant noise experienced over a long period of time can affect your sleep patterns, reduce your ability to concentrate, and inhibit your ability to take in new information or learn new skills.

TRAFFIC POLLUTION
Traffic, and the pollution it causes, not only affects your mood, increasing anxiety and stress levels, it can also result in premature death. Scientists in Germany have found a correlation between traffic jams and heart attacks. Research reveals that you are three times more likely to suffer a heart attack within an hour of being in a traffic jam than those who have not been stuck. Chronic stress is well known as a factor in heart disease, but this research indicates that chronic stress sufferers are more than twice at risk when exposed to traffic pollution, whether in a car, on public transport, or as a cyclist.

Diet and stress

Food is fuel. We need to eat the correct combination of food types – vitamins, minerals, fibre, fats, sugars, proteins, carbohydrates, and so on – in order to function optimally and so that our food intake matches our energy output. If it were up to our bodies to decide what we ate and when, there would be very few eating disorders and the epidemic level of obesity blighting the futures of so many people would not exist. In the United States, probably the most health-conscious country in the world and the one with the disposable income to do something about it, current levels of obesity are running at about 60 per cent of the population.

THE STRESS EFFECT

Rather than being motivated strictly by need, what we eat more often than not is the result of habit, mood, advertising, ready availability, as a reward, and, not surprisingly, stress. Anxiety, low self-esteem, tension, and the other outward manifestations of stress lead to such common eating disorders as over- and undereating, food bingeing, comfort eating, and the use of food as a distraction, a displacement activity to avoid confronting crises or upsets.

The way we respond to stress has an even more profound effect, as its onset also triggers strong desires for particular types of food, such as highly flavoured, instant-reward, high-fat chocolate, biscuits, and full-fat crisps, as well as caffeine-rich tea, coffee, and cola (see p. 21). The energy we derive from these foods is high and immediate, though it is depleted

THE IMPORTANCE OF WATER
Health professionals recommend that we drink a minimum of 2 litres (3 pints) of plain water each day. Use water as a substitute for stress-inducing caffeine-containing drinks, such as coffee and cola.

just as rapidly, leaving us with the type of blood-sugar swings that is very likely to lead to overeating, weight gain . . . and increased stress.

HEALTHY EATING
It can be difficult to eat healthily and well when you lead a busy life and are pushed for time. But rather than consider meal times a chore, try to think of food as a pleasure you can indulge in three times every day.

Good food is not necessarily complicated food. Choose your ingredients with care and aim to eat locally sourced, fresh, seasonal fruit and vegetables, organically grown if possible, as well as a balanced mix of complex carbohydrates and proteins, from animal or vegetable sources (see right).

WHAT TO EAT
- *Eat at least the five recommended portions of fruit and vegetables every day.*

- *Eat a good range of complex carbohydrates, including brown and wild rice, oats, wholemeal pasta, potatoes, and wholemeal bread.*

- *For protein, eat pulses, nuts, white meat (predominantly), oily fish, and soya products.*

VEGETABLES

Vegetables eaten raw contain the maximum amount of goodness, though make sure they are thoroughly washed and, if non-organic, peeled as well. If cooking, steam or boil as briefly as possible.

FRUIT

Grazing on fruit is a healthy alternative to snack bars and desserts. Wash all fruit thoroughly before eating and it is best to peel non-organic types. Fruit can also be lightly stewed and flavoured with spices.

WHAT NOT TO EAT

- *Limit your intake of red meat, full-fat cheese, milk, and other dairy products.*

- *Cut added salt down to a bare minimum. It will take a week or two to lose the taste for salt, but once it's out of your system you can start enjoying the real taste of food once more.*

- *Avoid "ready meals", which are usually packed with colourings and preservatives, including salt. The sugar content of these meals is also often very high to disguise the taste of the salt. Other types of convenience foods can also increase the toxin levels in your system, adding to the stress you are feeling. So watch your intake of dehydrated, tinned, and packet foods.*

- *Tea, coffee, sodas, and colas are often loaded with caffeine. Drink decaffeinated types or, better still, caffeine-free herbal teas or plain water.*

- *Limit your consumption of alcohol.*

FISH AND MEAT

Lean meat is best for your health, so remove excess fat (and the skin from chicken) before grilling, roasting, or baking. Fish benefits from being lightly steamed, grilled, or baked.

GRAINS AND PULSES

These represent a very useful and tasty source of carbohydrates, fibre, and proteins. This food group makes up a crucial part of a vegetarian diet.

FLAVOURINGS

Herbs and spices flavour foods, complementing and highlighting the natural taste of the ingredients. They can also make quite ordinary fare taste special. More than that, herbs and spices create wonderful aromas while the food is cooking, raising our expectation of the enjoyment of the coming meal.

HEALTHY DRINKS

If you need a concentrated infusion of vitamins, minerals, and essential trace elements you will go a long way to do better than a glass of fresh vegetable or fruit juice. As ever, the quality of the raw ingredients determines the goodness in the juice you get out, so buy good-quality, preferably organically grown, produce and wash it thoroughly before use to remove any traces of pesticides or fertilizers. Non-organic produce is best peeled, if possible, though you do then run the risk of removing much of its nutritional value, which is often concentrated just under the skin. If using tinned fruit, buy the type preserved in fruit juice rather than a sugar-rich syrup.

All fruit and vegetable drinks are best prepared and drunk fresh. However, juice made in the morning for, say, consumption at lunchtime is no problem. Pour the juice into a thermos flask and keep it sealed in a refrigerator until required.

Smoothies

These popular drinks are made by blending milk or yoghurt with various types of fruit. As well as tasting wonderful, smoothies are nutritious and they can also count toward the essential five portions of fruit and vegetables you should be eating daily (see p. 25). If you are worried about the amount of full-fat dairy in your diet, use low-fat milk or yoghurt, or sheep's or goat's milk products. For vegans, also suitable are soya milk, rice milk, and almond milk. Bear in mind that you need some fat in your system for the absorption of such vitamins as A and D, as well as minerals such as calcium, which are all fat soluble.

USING A JUICER OR BLENDER

Juicers are intended to extract as much of the liquid content of the fruit or vegetables as possible, while leaving the pulp behind. Blenders, however, break down all of the material to produce a thick, smooth-textured liquid. It is the inclusion of the whole fruit or vegetable, fibre and all, that makes blended ingredients so health-giving. The juice alone does not count toward your essential five daily portions.

PREPARING HERBAL TEA

With dried ingredients, use about 2 heaped teaspoons of leaves in 600ml (1 pint) of water; use 4 teaspoonfuls of fresh leaves. Cover with boiling water in a teapot and allow to stand for between 10 and 15 minutes.

If you are using the bark, seeds, stems, or roots, simmer the ingredients in a pan for between 10 and 15 minutes before straining the liquid into a cup and sweetening it with honey to taste.

Tea

This popular drink is consumed in one form or another in most countries of the world. However, due to the caffeine content found in some of the most common types, you might want to consider switching to one of the stress-reducing herbal teas for at least some of your tea consumption.

Valerian tea has a mild tranquillizing effect, though you might need to use a sweetener, such as honey, to help with the taste. Tea made from St John's wort can be used to help with the symptoms of mild depression, while chamomile tea is a great aid to relaxation. Kava kava tea may be difficult to find, but it is popular in some countries for its anxiety-reducing properties. There is also a wide range of tasty, caffeine-free fruit teas commonly available.

PROBLEM EATING

Eating the right types of food plays a crucial part in any strategy to combat stress. The trouble is that when you are caught up in the whirlwind of conflicting emotions that often accompanies this condition, are you able to make the right food decisions? Planning ahead is the key. The following points will help if over- or undereating is your concern, while the chart (see opposite) gives you an indication of what your weight ought to be.

If overeating is your problem

- Make a note of what you eat and when and where you eat it to see if you can identify any pattern in your eating. If, for example, you always eat a bag of crisps while waiting for the television news to start, go for a walk instead to break the routine.

- Don't keep any of the foods you are too fond of in a desk drawer at work or in the refrigerator at home.

- Don't watch the television or read a newspaper while eating. Instead, concentrate on the food and savour its flavour, texture, and aroma. Allow a good 10 minutes after eating a meal before deciding to have a second portion. This gives your stomach time to register the food and to feel full.

- Eat fruit snacks or small quantities of unsalted nuts as a reward or to prevent you feeling over-hungry. If food cravings get on top of you, then you are likely to binge on the wrong type of food.

- Don't go food shopping when feeling under pressure and stressed. The temptation is too great to fill the cupboards with high-sugar, deep-fried, low-fibre, caffeine-laced, stress-inducing junk foods.

- If you do weaken, go for the small packet of crisps and ignore the 33 per cent extra free offer on the family-sized bar of chocolate.

If undereating is your problem

- If confronting a full-sized meal is your problem, eat small amounts of nutritious food throughout the day.

- As well as being stress-reducing in its own right, physical exercise (see pp. 32–7) also acts as a spur to appetite. Exercise need not be vigorous – just get off the bus two stops early and walk the rest of the way.

- Keep a container of raisins or other dried fruit or seeds and nuts readily to hand so if you do feel like snacking, you will have something healthy and tasty to eat.

- Hot foods often have more flavour and certainly more aroma than cold foods, and so they may be more tempting for you to try.

- Do not overfill your plate at mealtimes. Try just a little of each of the different foods that are on offer and if your appetite returns later, rely on your healthy snack options rather than eating junk food.

- A bowl of homemade soup or a nutritious smoothie (see p. 28) may be easier to face than a plate of food.

WEIGHT RANGES
This weight-range chart makes no gender distinction, as insurance statistics indicate that weight alone does not alter the risk factors for men and women of equal height.

HEIGHT (m/in)	WEIGHT (kg/lb)	HEIGHT (m/in)	WEIGHT (kg/lb)
1.45 (57)	42–53 (92–116)	1.72 (68)	59–74 (130–163)
1.48 (58)	42–54 (92–119)	1.74 (69)	60–75 (132–165)
1.50 (59)	43–55 (95–121)	1.76 (69)	62–77 (136–169)
1.52 (60)	44–57 (97–125)	1.78 (70)	64–79 (141–174)
1.54 (61)	44–58 (97–127)	1.80 (71)	65–80 (143–176)
1.56 (61)	45–58 (99–127)	1.82 (72)	66–82 (145–180)
1.58 (62)	51–64 (112–141)	1.84 (72)	67–84 (147–185)
1.60 (63)	52–65 (114–143)	1.86 (73)	69–86 (152–189)
1.62 (64)	53–66 (116–145)	1.88 (74)	71–88 (156–194)
1.64 (65)	54–67 (119–147)	1.90 (75)	73–90 (160–198)
1.66 (65)	55–69 (121–152)	1.92 (76)	75–93 (165–205)
1.68 (66)	56–71 (123–156)	1.94 (76)	76–95 (168–209)
1.70 (67)	58–73 (127–160)	1.96 (77)	78–97 (172–214)

Exercise

The fact that a sensible amount of regular exercise is good for your physical health will probably come as no surprise. However, exercise is also good for your mental wellbeing, influencing your ability both to cope with and to manage stress and anxiety.

Remember that you are more likely to maintain any type of exercise regime if you positively enjoy it, so pick the form of activity that suits you best and is fun. You may, for example, feel happier exercising alone – jogging, say, or working out alone at the gym. Others, however, might benefit from the discipline of a structured exercise class where you can share your progress with others.

THE BENEFITS TO YOU

A single regular exercise session is reckoned to release enough of the natural morphine-like endorphins into

AS YOU LIKE IT
All forms of exercise – from gentle jogging and jumping rope to bicycle riding – can help alleviate at least some of the symptoms of stress. Apart from the benefits it brings to your cardiovascular and immune systems, exercise is a very effective distraction, perfect for taking your mind off your worries.

the brain to alter mood for as long as two hours. In addition, physical exertion helps to burn off the stress hormones released into the bloodstream as a result of the "fight-or-flight" response to stressful situations (see pp. 14–15). As well, exercise helps to restore proper digestion and produces a lower resting heart rate. And many studies have also shown that regular exercise helps people deal with the effects of depression compared with those who do no exercise at all. A reduction in feelings of anxiety could be another of the benefits of regular exercise helping to combat one of its major and most disruptive symptoms – broken and disturbed sleep (see pp. 42–3).

TYPES OF EXERCISE
If you have not exercised for a good period of time, if you are older than about 30 years, or have recently

A PROPER PERSPECTIVE
It is possible to become so dependent on your daily "fix" of exercise that if for some reason – through illness, say – you cannot participate in your usual exertions, your stress and anxiety levels may actually increase sharply and remain elevated until you resume your normal routine.

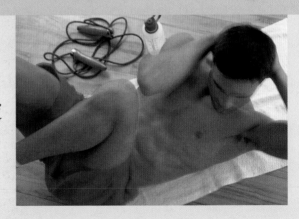

A SOLITARY THING
A solitary workout at home or at the gym is preferred by some people. Paying for gym membership in advance, however, might make it more likely that you attend to your exercises on a regular basis.

suffered with any type of illness, it is wise to consult your doctor before starting to exercise. Even if you have no medical anxieties, start any new exercise programme slowly, building up your stamina and fitness progressively as your body becomes stronger.

The three main types of exercise are aerobic, anaerobic, and sports exercise – though you are likely to find elements of more than one type in any particular exercise activity.

Aerobic exercise

This type of exercise involves any activity that increases your breathing and heart rate over an extended period. It requires the heart and lungs to work harder than normal and you can probably continue for between 20 and 45 minutes without feeling exhausted. At some point in this, the body has to "burn" its fat reserves to maintain the activity.

The main benefits you derive from aerobic exercise – such as jogging, bicycling, karate, stair climbing, rowing, swimming, fast walking, and rollerblading – is that it increases the efficiency of the cardiovascular and respiratory systems, bolsters the immune system, bolsters self-image and helps alleviate feelings of stress and anxiety.

Anaerobic exercise

This type of exercise is very different. Rather than being slow, fat-burning in nature, the effectiveness of anaerobic activity depends on short, intense bursts of exertion, the type that leave you gasping for air, followed by rest periods. This form of exercise can only be performed for a minute or so at a time as it depends on the limited amount of glycogen that is

GROUP ACTIVITIES
Being part of an exercise class (see opposite) means you receive guidance from a qualified teacher. And, if all goes well, you may even develop a new circle of friends. If nothing else, the competition may make you work harder to achieve your fitness goals – though keep the competition friendly unless you want your stress levels to climb.

stored in the muscles being made available for burning. Once the glycogen is gone, severe muscle fatigue follows.

The main benefits to you from anaerobic exercise include an increase in your speed, strength, and power, an increase in muscle mass, and the types of stress-reducing improvements that come from physical activity and a bolstered self-image. Common types of anaerobic exercise are weight lifting, sprinting, push-ups, stomach crunches, and pull-ups.

Sports exercise

This is the type of exercise – some aerobic, some anaerobic – that you get from playing all manner of sport, such as basketball, tennis, badminton, soccer, football, golf, cricket and so on.

The major benefits you are likely to derive from sports exercise include an improvement in general body tone and wellbeing, better co-ordination, increased flexibility, and better balance.

SUPPLEMENTS
When you start burning energy through exercise, you need to take on board the right fuel. A balanced diet of complex carbohydrates, proteins, and essential fatty acids (see pp. 24–31) is crucial and you may also need to supplement your vitamins C, E, and beta carotene intake.

FUN EXERCISE
Virtually any type of physical activity, unless you carry it to extreme lengths, will do your physical and mental states a power of good. Even a friendly game of tennis three or four times a week will improve your general fitness and help you develop a more positive attitude to life.

YOGA FOR STRESS RELIEF

Yoga – and especially the breathing exercises such as alternate nostril breathing (see p. 94), as well as the corpse pose (see p. 129) – is an exercise system ideally suited to help in the management of stress and anxiety. Its combination of gentle, flowing movements, breathing training, meditation, and relaxation helps to engender a sense of harmony and wellbeing in the physical body and nervous system. In addition, yoga brings a sense of calmness and contemplation to mind and spirit.

As a prequel to a yoga exercise session intended to control stress and anxiety, spend between 5 and 10 minutes in the corpse pose – depending on the time you have available. This will relax you and help to distance you from the factors in your life that have caused you your present distress. It will also separate you from anything in the future that you may be fretting or concerned about.

If you find your mind dwelling on any of your stress-inducing concerns during the session, use the alternate nostril breathing exercise to still and quiet your mind.

Time management

There are simply never enough hours in the day. Time is of the essence. The tyranny of the clock.

Do these statements sound all too relevant to you and your situation? And even if you could magically pull an extra few hours a day out of thin air, would it really solve the problem? Or would you be in precisely the same situation a month or two down the line?

When there is too much to do during the normal working day, the first thing that is usually sacrificed in an attempt to lessen the stress is your personal time – the essential component of your life set aside for yourself, your family, and your friends. So before the stress and anxiety takes its toll on both your physical and mental wellbeing, take this opportunity to refine your time-management skills.

Success here depends on being able to make an objective assessment of what can realistically be achieved in any particular time frame and what cannot. If the task is impossible to get done, and you are not able to delegate all or some of it, say "No". Dump it from your schedule.

The objective of time management should be to achieve a good balance of work, home, leisure, and personal time. Fail in this objective and the burnout that ensues will result in a deterioration in your efficiency, leading to tasks taking longer than they ought, increased pressure from all sides, and most probably elevated stress levels.

Use the list opposite as a guide to see how you might improve the balance between all the competing demands you have on your time.

MANAGING YOUR TIME

- *Don't jump from one activity to another, leaving a trail of incomplete tasks in your wake.*

- *Set aside blocks of time to accommodate all the competing demands on your life – work, home, and leisure.*

- *Be realistic when assessing what can and cannot be achieved.*

- *Learn to say "No" if your experience tells you the task cannot be achieved in the allocated time.*

- *Learn to let go and delegate work to others if at all possible.*

- *Make lists of all the jobs that need to be done, prioritize them, and then allocate time for them in a diary especially set up for the task.*

- *Review your diary at specific times during the day, update it, and re-prioritize as necessary.*

CHAPTER TWO

Starting your day

Wake up after a disturbed night's sleep, stumble through your morning rituals fretting about the "horrors" awaiting you at work, eat a breakfast packed with refined carbs, and wash it all down with a mug or two of caffeine-rich tea or coffee. Is it any wonder when the day goes from bad to worse?

You can start the process of dismantling the stress in your life from the moment you open your eyes in the morning, because the way you are when you first get out of bed sets the tone for the rest of the day. Indeed, often the best approach is to start the reforming process the night before, using targeted visualizations intended to calm your thoughts and bring about a positive resolution to whatever is troubling you. Getting on top of that destructive downward spiral of stress producing tiredness, tiredness producing stress and so on, depends crucially on your morning routine.

There is a range of different therapies you can bring to bear on stress-related problems – most based either on making you feel more positive about yourself or on showing you how to see troubling situations from new perspectives. It is unlikely you will have sufficient time in the mornings to try all the therapies suggested in this chapter, but if you try them a few at a time, building up your speed and expertise over a period of weeks, you may find that you can make room for more and more.

And don't be disappointed if positive results are not immediate. After all, the problems you are now confronting have probably been building up for a number of years, so give yourself the space and time to learn new behavioural approaches and coping techniques.

Harnessing your sleeping mind

Every night you have the chance to let go of the stresses and anxieties of the day. However, without the activities of your waking life acting as a distraction, you may find your mind in a state of constant vigilance as scenes from the day play themselves out over and over again. And then that tormenting worm of restlessness in the pit of your stomach starts to demand your attention, not allowing you more than a few minutes' rest before you have to move an arm, a leg, flip onto your back, or change sides. As the minutes crawl by, with that delicious state of unconsciousness still eluding you, all you can think about is the little time there is left before the alarm shatters the quiet of the room.

And so a cycle is established – stress and anxiety leading to poor sleep, while increasing tiredness produces poor performance at work and additional stress and anxiety. You can, however, harness your sleeping mind to break this cycle and ease the distressing symptoms of stress.

CRYSTAL HEALING
Many crystals, such as those in the bowl beside the bed opposite, are used to relieve the symptoms of stress and anxiety. For the effects of stress, try amethyst, tiger's eye, peridot, aquamarine, calcite, rose quartz, and tourmaline. To encourage a relaxed frame of mind suitable for sleep, try choosing from moonstone, quartz (rose and smoky), amethyst, citrine, onyx, blue jade, selenite, and tourmaline, depending on what appeals to you.

TARGETED VISUALIZATION
Using visualization to create a state of calm can turn off the fight-or-flight mode (see pp. 14–15) and promote a sense of relaxation and wellbeing.

- Make yourself comfortable in bed and bring to mind some relaxing, sun-drenched scene. Try recalling a "still" from a holiday you really enjoyed. Concentrate on it and imagine the warmth on your skin, the feel of the breeze, and all the glorious scents it carries.

Bring all senses to bear on the scene for about 10 minutes before returning to the world around you.

- If there is something specific generating your feelings of anxiety, such as a problem at work, visualize a successful resolution to the situation.

- Every night before drifting off to sleep, see yourself dealing with the situation and feel your confidence grow as the pleasure this brings infiltrates itself into every part of your body.

- Reinforce this positive visualization at least 10 times before falling asleep, and repeat the entire process every night for at least a week.

Before you rise

Countering the effects of stress starts before you get out
of bed. Rather than the violent movement and jolt to
the nervous system of jumping up at the sound of the
alarm clock, take the extra time you need to ensure
body and mind get off to the best possible start.

The following exercises are designed as an
affirmation of your intention to pamper and cherish
yourself. This not only helps you to boost your sense of
wellbeing and strengthen your ability to cope with
life's daily pressures, but you will also have the
physical resilience necessary to roll with the punches.

MORNING STRETCHES

These stretching routines are typical of those you
would come across at pilates classes. Pilates is a
gentle, non-aerobic form of exercise that is designed
to produce a toned and mobile body combined with a
calm and relaxed mind.

BACK CARE
*If you have back problems,
take particular care with
your sleeping posture and
choose a firm, supportive
mattress and a pillow that
keeps your neck aligned with
the rest of your spine. The
foetal position is particularly
comfortable and if you have
lower back problems, use a
pillow, as shown, to support
the weight of your upper leg.*

FREEING UP YOUR LOWER BACK

You should try this simple exercise before getting out of bed in the morning. It is particularly beneficial if you carry a lot of stiffness in the lower back after a night's rest (often the result of a fluid build-up in that area during the night), but it is also a help in releasing tension throughout the back and neck and a great boon in improving your posture.

(01) Throw back the covers to give yourself complete freedom of movement. Lie flat on your back with knees bent and slightly apart. Tighten your stomach muscles and keep them tensed throughout. Lift your legs and clasp your knees.

(02) Breathe in and as you exhale pull your right knee as close as you can to your chest. Don't force the movement. Inhale and as you exhale pull your left knee to your chest.

(03) Take another breath and as you exhale pull both knees as close as you can to your chest. Repeat this sequence 10 times.

FREEING UP YOUR HIPS

This pilates exercise is designed to free up your hips and increase flexibility in the lower back. If you have any sensitivity in this region, take great care with this exercise.

(01) Lie flat on your back, knees raised and a shoulder-width apart, and with feet flat on the mattress (or floor).

(02) Inhale and then, as you exhale, swing both knees as low as you can to the right. Allow your left buttock to lift slightly to increase the movement. Turn your head to the left as you move your knees to the right. Inhale and, as you exhale, re-centre your knees and head. Next, repeat the movement on the left side. Repeat the exercise 5 times on each side, making 10 in total.

MUSCLE TONE AND POSTURE
By strengthening the abdominal muscles and lengthening the lumbar spine, you can make a huge improvement to your posture.

(01) Turn face down on the bed and place a small cushion between your thighs and support your stomach region with a normal-sized pillow. Support your head on your arms as shown or turn it to one side if that position is more comfortable.

(02) Breathe in and, as you exhale, bring your attention to bear on the cushion by squeezing the muscles in your buttocks. Try to keep your legs still. Relax your muscles and rest in this position for a few moments.

(03) Remove the pillow and cushion and draw your knees up under your chest. Stretch your hands out in front. Remain in this resting pose for a few minutes until you feel completely relaxed.

MEDITATIVE TECHNIQUES

Many forms of meditation require practitioners to make their mind a blank as a first step in their journey – an internal pilgrimage to a place of spiritual growth and enlightenment. However, after a disturbed night's sleep – sleep disturbances being a common symptom of elevated stress levels – emptying your mind of troublesome thoughts may be a tall order. Because of this, the type of meditation known as a visualization may be easier for you to achieve, and can be just as effective in bringing about a settled and calm start to your day.

A visualization is more informal than a meditation. Rather than blanking out your thoughts, you need to fill your mind with images of the positive outcome you desire. You may wish to tackle an important meeting, interview, or presentation that is coming up at work, for example, or visualize a successful outcome to a social or professional confrontation with a friend or colleague you have been dreading. You may, of course, desire a less-specific outcome from your visualization, simply wanting to regain a sense of inner peace and calm.

Learning to breathe properly is crucial. As you breathe in slowly, feel your chest expand as the air fills your lungs. Hold your breath for a few seconds and then start to exhale. Again, take your time, completely emptying your lungs. Before taking the next breath, pause for a few seconds. Continue to focus your attention on your breathing and after a minute or two you should be feeling calmer and more relaxed as the tension ebbs away. Now follow the visualization on the right, adapting its form to suit your circumstances.

CALMING MEDITATION

The form of this visualization is very versatile. You don't even need to get out of bed, as you can start as soon as you wake up.

- *Sit up comfortably in bed or lie down and relax. With your eyes closed, let your breath flow naturally in and out as described on the left. Embrace yourself by placing your left hand in the right armpit and your right hand in your left armpit.*

- *As a sense of peace arises from within, focus your attention on this feeling. Allow it to fill your whole being, pushing aside the troublesome thoughts that have disturbed your sleeping hours, leaving no room for anything apart from the smooth flow of your breath in and out.*

- *Stay with this feeling for as long as your morning schedule will allow you – aim for a minimum of 10 minutes.*

Sun salutation

This sequence of yoga movements, known as the sun salutation, or *surya namaskar*, increases your body's suppleness and strength when performed every day. It also encourages healthy, rhythmic breathing, and helps to dispel tension and anxiety. If you suffer from high blood pressure, however, don't lower your head below the level of your heart.

Each posture should link to the next to create a seamless, flowing movement. But don't think you have to be an expert to perform the sun salutation – just try to copy the poses shown below and opposite as closely as possible.

MOVEMENT SEQUENCE

(01) Stand in the prayer position, knees and feet together. Regulate your breathing by inhaling and exhaling once.

(02) Inhaling, raise your arms while arching your back from the waist.

(03) Exhaling, swing your upper body forward from the hips. Place your hands on the floor. Bend your knees if necessary.

(04) Inhaling, move into a lunge position by extending one leg backward. Arch your back if possible, lift your chin, and look up.

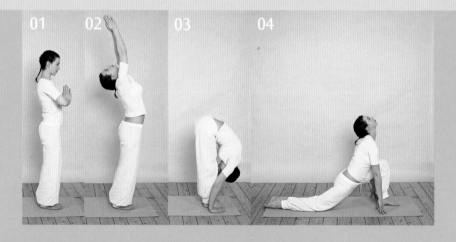
01 02 03 04

(05) While holding your breath, move your other leg back, forming the "plank" position.

(06) Exhaling, lower your knees to the floor and in stages lower your chest and forehead to the floor.

(07) Inhaling, lower your hips to the floor as you arch your back as deeply as you can. Lift your chin and look up.

(08) Exhaling, tuck your toes under and lift your hips to form the "dog" pose.

(09) Inhaling, move forward with one foot positioned between your hands. This is a mirror image to step 04.

(10) Exhaling, bring the other leg forward, come to your feet, and hinge forward from the waist, as in step 03.

(11) Inhaling, raise your arms while arching your back from the waist, as in step 02.

(12) Exhaling, slowly return to the standing prayer position, as in step 01.

Repeat this sequence, leading with the other leg, at least 3 times.

Follow your nose

With stress featuring as an associated risk factor in three of the top ten causes of death in developed countries, the beneficial effects of aromatherapy essential oils need consideration as part of a stress-busting strategy. Not only can these oils help you through specific crisis points, they can also tackle the chronic, dispiriting effects of stress.

EXPERIENCING ESSENTIAL OILS

One of the best ways to enjoy the benefits of essential oils is to heat a few drops in an oil burner (below right). The oil is mixed with water, which is heated by a candle in the base, and as the water vaporizes it carries the oil's aroma into the air. You can also smell concentrated oil directly from the bottle, but take care as some can be overwhelming. Ring burners fit around the top of a light bulb, and use the heat from the bulb to vaporize small quantities of oil. Vaporizers use steam to distribute the oil, while some people prefer to use oil misters. You first fill the mister with water, then add the recommended amounts and blends of oil, shake well, and spray. And when mixed with a carrier oil, some essential oils become suitable for massage.

IMPORTANT STRESS-REDUCING ESSENTIAL OILS

To counter such common stress-related disorders as tension, anxiety, and chronic mental fatigue, try:

- Sweet marjoram – good for reducing the effects of anxiety.
- Lavender – good for relaxation and relieving stress.

- Rosemary – aids concentration.
- Juniper berry – reduces anger and anxiety.
- Geranium – reduces feeling of stress and anxiety.
- Chamomile – reduces feelings of stress.
- Clary sage – aids relaxation.
- Sandalwood – relieves insomnia and depression.

SPECIFIC AILMENTS
The range of stress-related disorders that can potentially be helped by aromatherapy is wide:

■ Nervous tension – regulating and relaxing oils include basil, bergamot, cedarwood, chamomile, cinnamon, frankincense, geranium, lavender, marjoram, neroli, ylang ylang.

■ Anxiety and apprehension – calming oils include cedarwood, cypress, geranium, juniper, lavender, melissa, neroli, rose, thyme, ylang ylang.

■ Low self-esteem – boosting, reassuring oils include caraway, cedarwood, fennel, ginger, hyssop, juniper, laurel, pine, rosemary, tea tree, thyme.

■ Anger – pacifying oils include bergamot, chamomile, grapefruit, lavender, rose, yarrow.

■ Insomnia – calming, relaxing oils include basil, chamomile, lavender, mandarin, marjoram, melissa, neroli, rose, sandalwood, thyme, ylang ylang.

■ Depression – reassuring, uplifting oils include basil bergamot, chamomile, clary sage, grapefruit, lavender, melissa, neroli, orange, rose, sandalwood, thyme, yarrow, ylang ylang.

■ Interpersonal relations – oils for balance and friendship include caraway, fennel, geranium, ginger, juniper, lavender, marjoram, neroli, patchouli, peppermint, rose, ylang ylang.

■ Nervous exhaustion – oils that settle and regulate include basil, cinnamon, citronella, coriander, ginger, grapefruit, hyssop, jasmine, lavender, lemon grass, peppermint, nutmeg, rosemary, ylang ylang.

COLD WATER CURE?

Latest research suggests that stress levels could be reduced by the simple expedient of taking a cold bath or shower in the mornings. As part of the study into this approach, researchers subjected volunteers to a rigorous questioning session while their hands were plunged in cold water. Results suggested that this cold water approach encourages mental toughness, reduces measurable levels of stress, and stimulates the body's metabolic rate.

Breakfast

Our every instinct tells us that there is a strong and direct link between what we eat and our physical wellbeing. What might not be so obvious, however, is the connection between our food intake and our mental wellbeing.

When the body is suffering from undue levels of stress, requirements for certain nutrients alter. Food sensitivities in general also become more likely due to changes in the body's immune system. To ease the pressure on your system, you should start each day by shunning refined (highly processed) carbohydrates, while eating instead foods that are rich in fibre. The extra load stress places on your system also increases the need for vitamins B (particularly riboflavin), C, and E, as well as calcium, zinc, potassium, magnesium, and phosphorus.

If you simply find it impossible to shake off feelings of weariness first thing in the morning and cannot muster the enthusiasm or energy to rid yourself of those negative or gloomy thoughts, add in to the foods already mentioned those rich in the B group vitamins (particularly pantothenic acid, B12, and folic acid) and consider taking additional iron-rich foods (see pp. 25–7). This regime might also be beneficial if you are experiencing premenstrual syndrome or suffering from anaemia. If your tiredness persists or becomes worse, consult your doctor.

FOOD CHECKLIST
Breakfast dos
- *Citrus fruits*
- *Citrus fruit juices*
- *Bananas*
- *Dried fruits*
- *Pulses*
- *Nuts*
- *Lime flower, elderflower, chamomile, lemon balm teas*
- *Wholegrain cereals*
- *Wholegrain bread*
- *Milk*
- *Eggs*
- *Herrings*
- *Kippers*

Breakfast don'ts
- *Coffee*
- *Tea*
- *Cola*
- *Cocoa*
- *Added sugar*
- *Added salt*
- *Refined carbohydrates*

NLP

NLP, or Neuro-linguistic Programming, is a fast-acting technique developed in the 1970s by Americans Richard Bandler and John Grinder. NLP sessions are designed to show how you experience and understand the world and identify concerns, and help you develop techniques to bring about changes to your problem thought and behaviour patterns. An NLP approach to a situation causing you undue stress that may have occurred recently could follow along these lines:

- Replay the situation in your mind, remembering it in as much detail as possible, and paying particular attention to how the other person is responding to you – body language, gestures, and so on.

- With the insights gained from the first stage, replay the situation once more, this time experiencing it from the other person's perspective. Try to imagine what thoughts are going through that person's mind, what their emotional responses might be.

- Finally, imagine that you are an objective observer studying the situation as you replay the scene once more, and take note of any new insights that arise.

This exercise need take only a few minutes, but the process can be instrumental in giving you new insights into an upsetting situation and encourage you to have greater understanding of and empathy with the people you interact with at home and at work.

Centring meditation

Try to find time for this simple centring meditation
before starting work. It is designed to put you firmly in
touch with yourself and increase your focus on the here
and now. Centring can bring about a sense of great
calm and improve your ability to cope with panic,
anxiety, and stressful situations (see also page 48).

- Sit comfortably with eyes closed. As you slowly breathe
  in, feel your chest expand as the air fills your lungs.
  Hold your breath for a few seconds and then start to
  exhale. Again, take your time, completely emptying
  your lungs. Before taking the next breath, pause for
  a few seconds. Continue to focus your attention on
  your breathing for a minute or two.

- Move your attention to your feet and legs, becoming
  aware of how it feels where they make contact with
  the floor or chair. Feel, too, the contact your
  buttocks make with the surface beneath.

- Feel your spine rise up from the steadfast platform
  that is your pelvic region. Follow your spine up and
  up, becoming aware, in turn, of your torso, arms,
  shoulders, back, neck, and head. As you encounter
  tensions in muscles or joints, relax each one before
  moving onward and upward.

- Finish with your face and jaw, making sure no
  tension remains. Return your attention to your
  breathing for a minute or two, as in the first step.

CHAPTER THREE

Stress-free travel

Getting from A to B is, for most people, an uneventful transition. However, with transport becoming more sophisticated and widespread, more of us are being drawn into travelling further and further, for both work and leisure. As a result, stress is becoming an increasingly common travel experience.

Travel induces a range of reactions in people. Are you, for example, caught up in commuting to and from your place of work during the morning and evening rush hours? If so, it is not unusual for the daily struggle on crowded, dirty, and late-running buses or trains to reduce passengers to a state of mute fury. Or does your daily grind involve sitting behind the wheel of your car coping with traffic jams, roadworks, breakdowns, and the aggression and bad manners of your fellow drivers? It is not uncommon to spend up to 90 minutes on your daily commute into work and the same amount of time getting back home again. This works out at 15 hours – or an extra two working days – per week!

Rather than dwell on the more depressing aspects of public transport, you could instead use your time catching up on some pleasure reading. Or to take some of the pressure off your working day, why not make a start on that background reading you have been putting off or catch up on the news and gossip in your industry by reading your trade magazine or newspaper? Likewise, rather than endure the frustrations of all that wasted time behind the wheel, you can fill the car with calming aromatherapy fragrances and the soothing sounds of your favourite music. Though don't have the music so loud you cannot hear warning sounds from outside your vehicle.

And if your travelling involves a plane trip, you won't want to miss the advice on reducing the very real anxieties many people feel when it comes to flying (see pp. 72–5).

The daily grind

Ask a hundred people to choose the one thing from their working day they hate the most, and by a long way the answer you will get back is certain to be . . . the daily journey into work.

It could be stop-start traffic chaos that winds you up. Perhaps it's waiting at the side of the road despairing at the non-appearance of the bus that is so depressing. Or is it dirty, overcrowded, or late-running trains that send your blood pressure surging? Whatever it is, you can do something about it.

CHANGE YOUR SCHEDULE

The first thing you need to investigate is changing the time you leave home in the morning. By doing this, you may be able to avoid whatever it is causing you the stress.

For example, sometimes leaving half an hour earlier or later can make an enormous difference to the volume of traffic you encounter. Likewise, buses may be able to get through the traffic with less bother, and if there are fewer passengers on board as well, that's an added bonus. And getting to the train station just half an hour earlier or later may mean you get a seat. At least if you are not strap-hanging you are more prepared to overlook other shortcomings.

Discuss with your human resources department at work the possibility of flexi-time working, allowing you to vary your start and finish times just a little. Unless you are part of a team and the precise hours you work are critical to a particular process, you may find company procedures accommodating.

THE VICTORIOUS BREATH
One yogic breathing exercise (see also pp. 72 and 94) that is both simple and very effective at lowering stress levels is known as Ujjayi, or the victorious breath.

- *You will need to be seated while learning this exercise, but once it is familiar you can try it anywhere – in your car before setting off, on a bus, or strap-hanging on a train.*

- *As you breathe in deeply through your nose, the action is controlled by the muscles in the glottis. It is this that produces the hissing Ujjayi sound.*

- *Now breathe out very slowly through your nose, contracting the muscles around the glottis. The sound this time is rasping.*

- *Repeat this in- and out-breath sequence 6 times. Then breathe normally for 6 in- and out-breaths. This is one complete cycle, which you repeat 4 times.*

THE CALMING POWER OF CRYSTALS

Many crystals are useful for relieving stress and calming the mind during the daily grind to and from work, including aquamarine, tourmaline, and green calcite. However, if you want to feel more mentally in control, keep some amethyst in your pocket. Whenever you feel your control slipping, just hold them in your hand to feel your protective aura grow and expand.

CHANGE YOUR ROUTINE

Of course, if it is road traffic causing you grief then you might want to consider swapping to public transport. Certainly, people value the security, privacy, and comfort afforded by having their own cars, but you need to weigh up the pros and cons to see what really suits you best. It could be, for example, that by handing the responsibility of getting you to work over to somebody else, you could get some extra reading or report-drafting out of the way before even arriving for the day, so lessening the strain of your busy schedule. Or you may simply want to lose yourself in a book, listen to music on a personal stereo, or quietly meditate.

Make a list of all the things you appreciate about driving to work and then a corresponding list of all the drawbacks. Then do the same on another piece of

paper for your preferred form of public transport. Compare the two and then make your decision.

If you cannot kick the car habit completely, you could try car-sharing. At least this way you will be able to sit back and relax while somebody else does the driving on, say, a week-on, week-off basis. Advertise on noticeboards at work for drivers living close to you who might be interested in a car-sharing scheme.

Another way to beat the traffic is to walk or cycle. Both place the lowest possible strain on the environment, and the exercise may well help alleviate at least some of the symptoms associated with stress (see pp. 32–7).

REASSURING AROMAS

If you are prone to feelings of anxiety or desperation verging on panic, try this aromatherapy remedy:

- *Mix 3 drops of lavender and 2 drops of rose oil in 1 tablespoon of carrier oil.*

- *Transfer this to a tissue or handkerchief and, as soon as you feel the anxiety building, breathe the aroma in deeply.*

Behind the wheel

If you drive, especially during the morning or evening rush hours on your way to and from work, then you will know just what a frustrating and stress-making experience it can be. When it's not roadworks or faulty traffic light slowing things down, you also have to contend with the noise and pollution produced by your fellow drivers (see pp. 22–3). Tension and stress-induced headaches are all too common consequences.

DEALING WITH ROAD RAGE

In addition to these everyday driving issues, we have all experienced that burning nugget of anger in our bellies when another road user tailgates us with headlights flashing or cuts us up when lane changing, forcing us to give way. Combine this with the stress

RELEASE TENSION
(01) You only need a minute or so to interlace your fingers behind your head, with your palms cupping the back of your head.

(02) Relax your hands so that their weight pulls your head forward and down. Hold for 15–20 seconds and then breathe out, expelling all the air from your lungs. Bring your head up again and breathe normally. Repeat a few times, feeling the stretch in your neck and spine.

you may already be carrying with you from your home, personal, or work life and driving can become a very dangerous activity indeed.

Take notice of these feelings, as they might represent the early signs of road rage. This modern driving phenomenon is characterized by extreme anger and hostility leading to a desire for retaliation. Do something about it before things get out of hand:

- Don't allow other drivers to dictate your mood and behaviour. Responding aggressively yourself to the bad driving will only give the other person a measure of satisfaction.

- Realize that the other driver is not targeting you specifically with his or her bad driving – you are just in the wrong place at the wrong time.

- Let go of any feelings of anger that might be building. Preserving your serenity and peace of mind means that you will be feeling fine while the other driver is wound up tight.

- Try to empathize with the other driver. Think that perhaps something has gone disastrously wrong in that person's life.

- Put on some soothing music to help change your mood (see p. 70). And if you feel you may be losing it, pull over as soon as it is safe to do so and try some tension-release exercises (see opposite).

INCENSE CONES
Sandalwood incense, in the form of cones or sticks, is an ideal fragrance for driving, as it has a cooling and calming effect on the spirit. It can also calm an agitated emotional state and help to relieve tension headaches. Do not light the incense, however, as the smoke could be distracting and the fragrance overpowering in the confines of a car. Leave the incense unlit and allow its gentle aroma to permeate the entire space.

MUSIC TO SOOTHE THE SOUL

Music can soothe the soul and, more importantly, it can also calm the mind – and it is the intellect you need to engage if you want to stay safe behind the wheel. But take care not to become distracted by the need to change tapes, CDs, or stations while driving.

Not all music is a soothing accompaniment in the car. Some types can actually raise your heart beat and blood pressure – two of the body's natural responses to stress. To avoid this, follow the suggestions in these points:

- Studies suggest that to stay calm and composed you should listen to music with a rhythm that is slower than your heart rate.

- Avoid playing music that is particularly challenging or engaging – anything that takes your attention off the road is potentially dangerous.

- Music with a strong, rhythmic base beat can raise blood pressure and increase your heart rate. It can also lead on to more aggressive responses to other road users.

- Keep the volume at a reasonable level. As a guide, you should be able to talk to somebody sitting beside you without raising your voice. Very loud music distracts you and perhaps other drivers, too.

- You don't have to play anything as bland as muzak in the car, but try listening to something with a gentle, non-intrusive beat.

BE CALM, STAY SAFE

- Leave home with more than enough time for your journey. If you don't have to hurry, much of the tension will simply not exist.

- If you are travelling somewhere new, make sure you study the route before setting off. Not having to cope with a road atlas at the traffic lights makes for a stress-free journey.

- If you have children in the car, make provisions to keep them amused. Take some reading material for them, simple board games, or music they like.

- If stress levels start to increase, pull over and try the simple calming exercise opposite.

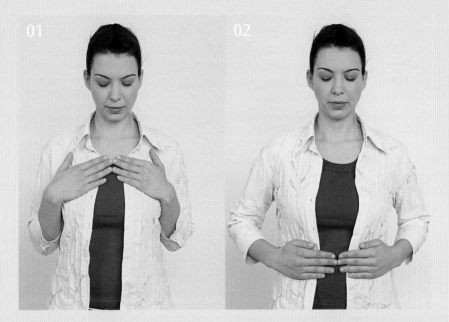

SETTLE YOUR EMOTIONS

Traffic problems can only get worse, at least for the foreseeable future. It is, therefore, a good idea to have a range of strategies at your disposal to help you through crisis points whenever they might arise. You will need to pull over and stop the car before trying this simple reiki exercise.

(01) Place your hands, palms flat to your body, on either side of your chest, as shown. Your fingertips should be touching just below the level of your collarbone. This helps to relieve you of negative emotions.

(02) Next, place the palms of your open hands over your ribcage, above the level of your waist. Again, your fingertips should just meet at the midline of your body. This position is very supportive, helping to reduce any feeling of frustration you may be experiencing behind the wheel. Hold each pose until you feel your mood change.

Air travel

Although for most of us air travel means the buzz of the challenge associated with a business trip or getting away somewhere exciting for a vacation or a new travel adventure, a significant number of people experience levels of anxiety ranging from mild apprehension through to debilitating phobia as the flight time draws near.

From my own experience I have found techniques that control and regulate my breathing (see right) to be the most effective in bringing down stress levels and stemming feelings of panic. And if your swallow reflex becomes difficult, especially on take-off and landing, sip plain water or fruit juice frequently to keep your throat relaxed and functioning properly.

GENERAL ADVICE

■ Take zinc supplements and echinacea before flying to boost your immune system, and up your intake of vitamin B complex to help with the effects of stress.

■ Leave for the airport with plenty of time to spare. Nothing increases anxiety and stress more than worrying about missing check-in times.

■ Don't drink caffeine-rich teas and coffees (see p. 21).

■ Limit your intake of alcohol. It may relax you in the short term, but other effects soon take over (see p. 20). In addition, on a long flight, the low oxygen level on board can make a hangover from drinking too much a more intense experience than usual.

REGULATE BREATHING
This yogic breathing exercise helps to relieve the symptoms of stress by inducing a sense of calm and relaxation, regulating your breath control, and producing a meditative state. (See also pp. 64 and 94.)

■ *Sit comfortably in your seat and direct your breath into the area of the upper chest.*

■ *Hold your breath for 2 sec and then breathe out.*

■ *Repeat 6 times.*

■ *Direct your breath into the ribcage, expanding your chest to accommodate it.*

■ *Hold your breath for 4 sec and then breathe out.*

■ *Repeat 6 times.*

Direct your breath deep down into the abdomen.

■ *Hold your breath for 6 sec and then breathe out.*

■ *Repeat 6 times.*

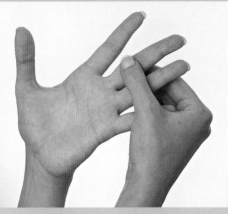

KEEP TABS ON STRESS

Deriving from the ancient Japanese therapy of jin shin, this easy, discreet exercise releases stress and allows you to let go of the anxiety that can be associated with flying. Firmly, but without undue pressure, hold the middle joint of your middle finger between the thumb and fingers of your other hand. Hold this position for a few minutes before repeating the exercise on your other hand.

CONTROL NERVOUS TENSION

Another jin shin exercise ideal for the air traveller helps to bring a sense of calm and a release of the nervous tension you may be experiencing. Firmly, but without undue pressure, hold your ring and little fingers between the thumb and fingers of your other hand, as shown. Hold this position for a few minutes before repeating the exercise on your other hand.

- Keep yourself well hydrated by drinking a variety of herbal teas, water, or fruit juices, and avoid eating salty snacks.

- Wear loose, comfortable clothing and walk around the plane as often as you can to lessen the risk of deep-vein thrombosis (DVT). Where space permits, try any exercises that help keep your circulation moving (see example on pp. 74–5).

HELP YOUR CIRCULATION
Unless you are lucky enough to fly business or first class, your experience of air travel is likely to be cramped. Try this pilates exercise at the back of the plane to ease circulation in stiff legs. It is a good idea to practise it at home first before trying it out in the air.

(01) Place your hands palm-side down on top of the seat back and bend your knees slightly.

(02) Tighten your stomach muscles and, with knees still bent and with a straight back, come up onto your toes as you breathe in. Hold this for a count of 5 seconds.

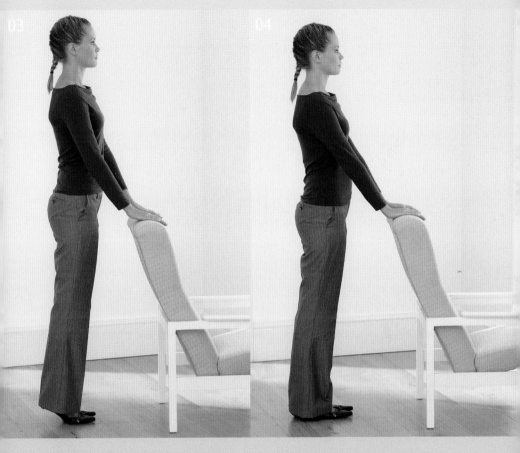

(03) *Keep up on your toes as you breathe steadily out and straighten your knees, rising up to your full height. Hold this position for a count of 5 seconds.*

(04) *Come down off your toes as you breathe in. Your back should still be straight and your coccyx centred and pointing directly downward at the floor. Breathe normally for a few seconds and then repeat this sequence up to 10 times.*

CHAPTER FOUR

De-stressing the working day

If you cannot change the circumstances that are
causing you stress at work, then you need to change
your attitude to the troublesome situation instead.
Learning to take control means that it is more likely
you will be able to defuse a stressful situation before
it can cause you harm.

If your work or the workplace is the root cause of your stress, you need to find a strategy for dealing with it. The first step is to identify the situations in which the stress arises. It could be that there are elements in the physical environment at work that are generating a stress response in you. In this respect, look at such things as noise levels, the types of lighting you habitually work under, air quality, pollution, and seating. Individually or in combination, these are all capable of causing headaches, migraines, and a whole range of specific physical ailments or just a generalized feeling of ill health.

The stress you are experiencing, however, could be the result of the personal baggage you are taking to work. Perhaps you are experiencing problems with your sleeping (see pp.42–3) or with your diet (see pp. 24–31); or it could be that it is the journey into work that is stressing you (see pp. 62–75). Maybe problems are arising through issues of low self-esteem, or perhaps some other common factor – such as money worries or problems with the children – or combination of factors is responsible (see pp. 20–23).

Another potential source of workplace stress is the friction that can stem from personality clashes with difficult colleagues, office politics, worries about career prospects, and, of course, the very real prospect for many people these days of redundancy as organizations "downsize" staffing levels and "outsource" the work.

Organizing your desk

It is almost too obvious to say, but since clutter causes stress, a clear and decluttered working space could be the starting point for a clear and clutter-free frame of mind, and so less stress. Putting away in their proper places all those essential components of your work – letters, diaries, printouts, memos, or all the things that relate to your occupation – as well as all the stuff that is simply junk – coffee cups, food wrappers, carrier bags, newspapers, and so on – is a good start in calming an agitated mind and soothing the stresses and tensions of the workplace.

FENG SHUI

Using the principles of the ancient Chinese art of feng shui, it is possible to organize your immediate working environment to bring about positive outcomes for yourself and your business. Feng shui can also help you to clear away the petty aggravations that are a part of all our lives. Coming from the Chinese for wind (*feng*) and water (*shui*), the practice involves the most auspicious arrangement of specific items in order to increase harmony and assist the flow of *chi*, or energy. Get this right and good fortune is certain to follow.

An integral part of feng shui is the use of tokens and symbols to attract auspicious luck or to repel or disperse ill-omens. For example, the use of crystals or semi-precious stones encourages others to be supportive of you, while the legendary three-legged toad is a powerful symbol for attracting wealth and success. It can be usefully placed on your desk or wherever it is you conduct business.

CREATIVE ENDEAVOUR
To make your desk into an engine of creative endeavour, take the following points into account.

- *If you are acquiring a new desk, choose one that does not have any sharp corners – rounded shapes are more auspicious.*

- *A crystal paperweight, or one made from a semi-precious stone, can help to sharpen your intuition. Place the paperweight at the back of the desk, in the centre.*

- *Place two yellow flowers in a vase in the top right-hand corner of your desk. This will help to make relations with work colleagues stress free.*

- *In the right-hand corner of your desk place a figure of the three-legged toad. This creature is known as the "money toad" and is depicted sitting on top of a pile of "lucky" money.*

Stress-proofing your working space

The average working space is far from a healthy environment. In an office, for example, you are likely to be in close proximity to a number of computer terminals, photocopiers, fax machines, electronic printers, and a host of other electrical equipment all producing stress-inducing electromagnetic fields (EMFs). Symptoms associated with EMFs include headaches, insomnia, high blood pressure, mood changes, and general poor health.

In addition, the office floor is likely to be covered in synthetic carpet treated with a range of chemical finishes; the walls coloured with paints emitting volatile organic compounds (VOCs); and shelving and desks made from particleboard giving off formaldehyde and other potentially harmful gases used during the manufacturing process.

Lighting is another area that often requires some thought. No matter where you work you are probably reliant on artificial illumination, such as fluorescent tubes or tungsten-halogen bulbs. Both types of lighting emit only partial spectra and so have colour biases, or casts. Your brain is quite capable of correcting these colour inaccuracies so that you see them correctly, but prolonged exposure, especially if you are doing close, detailed work, can be a contributing factor in headaches and migraines (see pp. 82–3).

Finally, the quality of the air you breathe in the workplace is often endlessly filtered and recirculated. This mechanical system can, at best, produce an unpleasant stale quality in the air or, at worst, become a breeding ground for germs and bacteria.

PUT THINGS RIGHT

- *Turn your computer off when it is not in use.*

- *If possible, position photocopiers, printers and other electronic equipment is a separate room where people do not work.*

- *Floors should be covered in cork or linoleum tiles rather than carpets and, as far as possible, all shelving, desks, and other furniture should be made from sustainably grown real wood. Everything should be decorated using low-odour natural paints.*

- *Position desks as close as possible to sources of natural light and open windows to reduce dependence on mechanical air-conditioning systems.*

- *Use plants not only as decorative features, but also to help purify the air.*

- *Black tourmaline, fluorite, and lapidolite can prevent the stress of EMFs.*

Headaches and migraines

There can be a range of causes of headache and migraine in the workplace. One of the most common – and also one of the most easy to remedy – is failing to drink sufficient water, resulting in dehydration (see p. 24). EMFs (see p. 118) are another common cause of headache, as are stress and anxiety.

We all recognize the situation; you are minutes away from a major presentation, crucial meeting, or a make-or-break sales pitch. You can feel the panic starting to mount and your stomach is knotting. You look down to find your hands clenched and your palms slicked with perspiration. There it is – the glimmer of a headache has just appeared.

No matter what the cause, before the headache can take hold try these simple techniques to bring relief from the tension and anxiety.

SELF-HELP REFLEXOLOGY
People most often associate reflexology with the feet, but it can also be used as a self-help technique on the hands.

(01) Dry your hands if sweaty and, using your left thumb, inch across the palm of your right hand as indicated. Keep your thumb in contact with your hand at all times. Start at the heel of the hand and work toward the fingers.

(02) Dry your hands again if necessary. This time use your right thumb to work steadily and methodically across the palm of your left hand.

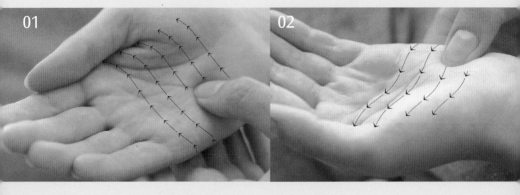

FACIAL MASSAGE

The pain you experience with a migraine is the result of blood vessels in the brain constricting, thus reducing the flow of blood. It is not uncommon for the veins in your temples to become more prominent than usual during one of these episodes.

(01) Dry your hands if they are sweaty and, using your middle fingers, gently massage your temples in a circular motion. You will know how much pressure to apply by the relief you feel it brings you.

(02) Using the same circular technique, extend the facial massage to take in the area of your eyebrows and around your eyes to the tops of your cheek bones. Massage in this fashion for at least 3 minutes – longer if time permits.

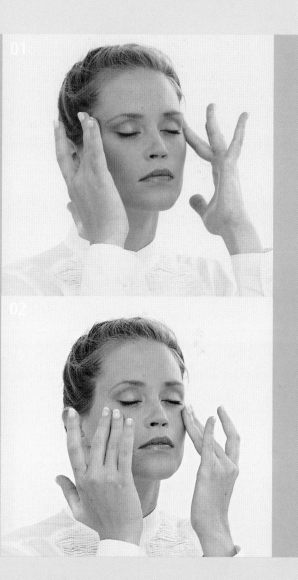

EYE STRAIN

Another common cause of headache and migraine can be put down to problems with your eyes, often exacerbated by working for long hours doing close work under poor lighting conditions or working without a break at a computer (see pp. 80–1). Take sensible precautions to safeguard your eyesight by working with natural light whenever possible and taking a break every 20–30 minutes. This might involve doing some simple eye exercises, such as focusing on objects at varying distances, including the far distance, taking a few minutes to try the relaxing facial exercises shown here, or try bathing tired eyes in an elixir made from gems, such as topaz, aquamarine, or jadeite.

Place a clean gem in a clean bowl of pure spring water in bright sunlight for at least 12 hours. Pour the water into a dark-coloured dropper bottle, diluted further with 50 per cent pure spring water to make an elixir. Use 1 or 2 drops in each eye to bring relief.

ACUPRESSURE MASSAGE

Try this sequence of acupressure exercises whenever your eyes feel strained and tired and you are concerned a tension headache may be building.

(01) Make your hands into cups and cover your eyes for 1–2 minutes. Make sure no light can creep through your fingers, but you need not put any pressure on the eyes themselves.

(02) Imagine that you are looking straight ahead and press the points above your eyebrows in line with the pupils. Exert light pressure with your index fingers for 30 seconds.

(03) *Exerting the same light pressure with your index fingers, now activate the acupressure points in the hollows found on either side of the bridge of your nose. Hold this for 30 seconds.*

(04) *Gently pinch the top of your nose just below your eyebrows, using your finger and thumb, and then pull down with an even pressure right to the tip of your nose.*

(05) *With both of your index fingers, press upward using a firm, steady pressure under your cheek bones. Hold this position for 30 seconds.*

(06) *To finish off this approximately 5-minute routine, repeat step 01, cupping your hands over your eyes to exclude all light for 1–2 minutes.*

Back and neck strain

Your body registers stress in a number of ways. Physical signals that stress may be a problem for you include poor sleeping patterns (see pp. 42–3), chronic stomach disorders, often the result of the "fight-or-flight" response (see pp. 14–17), and persistent headaches and migraines (see pp. 82–5). In addition, the types of muscular aches and pains associated with stress and anxiety are typically responsible for a range of muscular-skeletal problems, including backache, a tight or clenched jaw or other facial tensions, painful shoulders or, in extreme cases, a "frozen" shoulder, and a stiff, uncomfortable, immobile neck.

If these ailments are ignored and left untreated for any length of time, they simply feed directly back into the stress cycle, deepening and intensifying the problem. In this situation, the stress leads to physical complaints that increase feelings of inadequacy or an inability to cope, which then deepen the stress response, and so it goes. Try the exercises shown here, and those on pages 88–91 to help break this pernicious cycle.

LOOSENING THE NECK
(01) Roll your head clockwise and then counterclockwise 3 times in each direction.

HEAD AND NECK
(01–03) Drop your head until you feel a stretch. Then drop your head to each side and finally backward as far as it will comfortably go. Repeat this 10 times.

(02) Turn your head slowly from side to side 10 times and then 10 more times as quickly as is comfortable.

SIT WELL

To prevent common postural problems always sit with your feet flat on the floor (see right), keeping your back straight, and your lumbar spine supported by the chair back. For maximum benefit, your hips should be slightly higher than your knees. And if working at a computer screen, keep your head upright and level.

LOOSENING THE SHOULDERS

(01) Shrug each shoulder alternately 10 times. You should feel a pull from the muscles on the top of your shoulders each time.

(02) Shrug both shoulders together. Raise them high and allow them to drop down heavily. Repeat this 10 times. Keep a good straight spine and don't let your back sag.

EYES AND JAW

Your face will benefit from some relaxation exercises as much as any other part of your body.

(01–02) Screw your eyes tightly closed so that the surrounding muscles really bunch up. Then open them wide and relax your face. Repeat this 5 times.

(03–04) Slide your jaw firmly from side to side, extending it as far it will go. Next let your lower jaw sag down as far as possible. Repeat both movements 10 times.

OPENING THE SHOULDERS

Once you have loosened up your shoulders and got rid of the worst of the stiffness (see opposite), try this next sequence to bring further relief and extra freedom of movement.

(01) Allow your head to fall gently forward as you cross your lower arms as they rest in your lap. Breathe normally.

(02) Making a movement like slipping a shirt off over your head, breathe in and lift your arms up and over, as shown. Arch your back as far as you can and look up at the ceiling.

(03) Throw your arms wide with your fingers outstretched. As you breathe out, circle your arms and bring them down into the original starting position in your lap. Breathe normally for a few seconds and then repeat the sequence of movements 5–10 times.

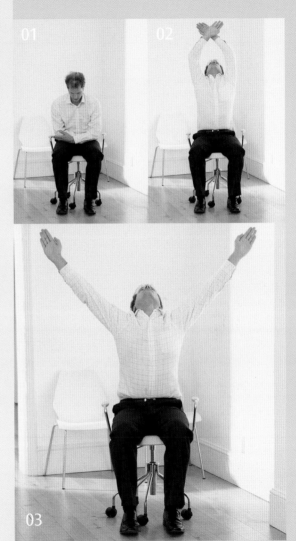

LOOSENING THE SPINE

This sequence of movements will help to loosen the middle area of your back, known as the thoracic spine. Try this whenever your have been sitting too long at your desk and your body is beginning to feel stiff and locked-up.

(01) Pull back from your desk and sit up straight in your chair. Lift your arms to chest level and bring your hands toward each other so that the fingers are just touching. Breathe normally.

(02) Take a breath in and, as your breathe out, swivel your upper body to the left from the waist. Pause in this position for 1–2 seconds with fingers still touching.

(03) Now take a breath in and, as you breathe out, stretch your left arm out and back as far as possible. If you can, swivel your body further while doing this. As you breathe in, bring your arm back to the middle, fingers touching once more. Do the same for the right side and repeat the whole sequence 10 times.

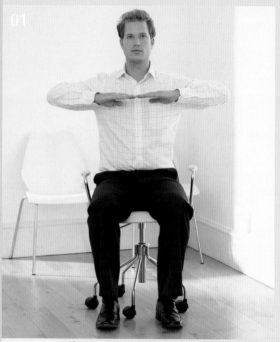

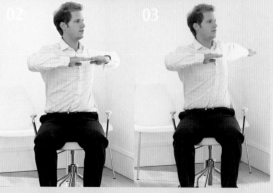

SPINAL SIDE STRETCH

In addition to the thoracic spine exercise shown opposite, try this sequence. Repeat it a total of 10 times.

(01) Place the palm of your right hand against the side of your ribs, high up, close to the area of your armpit. Stretch your left arm up as high as you can.

(02) On an out-breath, arch over to the right, bringing your arm over your head. Turn your head to the right. On an in-breath, return to the start position. Repeat for the other side.

Dealing with a difficult colleague

Most of us spend our waking hours either at work or travelling to and from it; as a result, we may well spend more time with colleagues than we do with family or friends. It's not surprising, then, that the workplace – with its built-in financial concerns, status considerations, and performance pressures – can become a fertile breeding ground for tense relationships. These can easily lead to elevated levels of stress that may get out of hand and tip over into conflict (see pp. 16–17).

Today, of all days, you need everything to go smoothly. A vital presentation is getting its first airing in a few hours and your key team member is late. This doesn't surprise you – tension between you has been high. None of us likes giving up evenings and weekends, but when the pressure's on, everyone has to make sacrifices. Looking out, you've just seen him in the car park. It's as though he's winding you up; sauntering in 40 minutes late. And there's still so much left to do!

Stop! Not only does this way of thinking achieve nothing, apart from making the stomach pains, indigestion, and headaches just that little bit worse, it certainly doesn't help you to achieve your goals – and it may not even reflect your true feelings about your colleague. First, try to see the situation from the other person's perspective (see p. 58). Even if you don't agree with them, you need to recognize their right to an opinion. Try these simple stress-busting techniques before the situation deteriorates.

LAVENDER ROOM MISTER
To bring about a successful resolution to a tense situation, add lavender essential oil to water in a room mister. Follow the directions on the label or add just 2 drops of essential oil. Spray the room a few minutes before a likely confrontation to allow time for the aroma to permeate the entire space.

Caution
Do not use lavender essential oil during the first trimester of pregnancy.

FLOWER TREATMENT

As an added measure to help you calm a tense situation, try placing 2 drops of beech flower remedy under your tongue (right). The qualities of the beech flower lessen your over-critical tendencies and so remove some of the potential causes of conflict between you and your colleague. Alternatively, try putting a few drops of calming pine essential oil on a tissue and sniffing it, as shown below right.

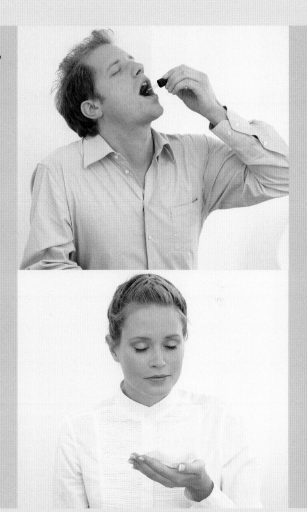

BREATHE RIGHT

When your stress levels are elevated, one of the first symptoms you notice is that your breathing becomes shallow and rapid. Accompanying this is a tightness in the chest, as if your body were being prepared for physical conflict. Indeed, that is exactly what is happening as the primitive "fight-or-flight" reflex kicks in (see pp. 14–15). Once you learn to recognize the symptoms, simple yogic breathing exercises, like those below, can help restore your body's equilibrium, bring about a state of calm, and so lessen the stress.

ALTERNATE NOSTRIL BREATHING
(01) Using your right thumb, press your right nostril closed and inhale through your left nostril for a steady count of eight. As you breathe in, imagine both lungs, right to the very bottom, inflating fully and your ribs expanding. Now close your left nostril, too, by placing your right index finger against it and hold your breath for another count of eight.

(02) Remove your thumb and breathe out fully through your right nostril to a steady count of eight. Draw your diaphragm in during this process to completely empty your lungs. Keeping your index finger against your left nostril, breathe in through your right nostril to a steady count of eight to complete one sequence. Repeat the sequence a total of 5 times.

BREAKING THE CIRCUIT

Once the adrenal glands kick in and start pumping adrenaline into your bloodstream, your stress levels are likely to take off. And as you become increasingly tense, so adrenaline levels rise still further. This is a stress-inducing circuit that definitely requires intervention. Even minor annoyances can trigger this physiological reaction, so it's not surprising that weeks of simmering conflict with your colleague has your teeth clenched, head throbbing, and hands tightened into fists. Try the calming reiki positions below.

CALMING INTERVENTION
(01) Stand with your hands open, covering your kidneys. This pose helps to calm the adrenal glands, which produce sex hormones and other hormones that help to control heart rate and blood pressure.

(02) To reduce the stress that has already built up, place your open hands over your eyes, with the palms covering your cheekbones.

(03) Cup your hands over the sides of your head, with the heels of your hands over your temples and your fingers pointing toward the centre-parting line. This pose helps you to feel more balanced about work commitments and enhances your ability to enjoy life.

Preparing for a meeting or interview

Getting into the right frame of mind before an important meeting or interview is a crucial component in avoiding stress and anxiety. And the correct mental attitude will also maximize your chances of a successful outcome. Try the following stress-reducing tips and also try the chi kung technique shown here.

- Make sure you know how to get to the meeting or interview. Leave with plenty of time to spare so you don't have to worry about being late.

- Find out as much about the company – what it does, when it was founded, and so on – in advance.

- Practise likely interview answers out loud. This will reduce anxiety and increase self-confidence.

- Be aware of your own nervous habits, such as picking the quicks of your fingernails, and make a conscious effort to keep them under control.

- Cultivate a positive, energetic, confident manner. Answer questions with enthusiasm and avoid monosyllabic "yes" or "no" responses.

- Make eye contact with the people at the meeting or interview and pay attention to your body language. Open arm and hand gestures imply that you are engaged in the process. Arms crossed in front of your chest implies you are closed off and defensive.

STAND TALL
This chi kung exercise boosts your self-confidence by making you feel invigorated and powerful. It takes only a few moments, so find a private spot before the meeting or interview begins.

(01) Stand with your feet a shoulder-width apart and with your weight evenly distributed over both feet. Feel centred and rooted to the ground. When you are ready, bring your fingers together and point them downward at the floor.

01

(02) *Raise your arms straight out from the sides of your body, bringing them up to shoulder height. Then turn your palms upward, facing the ceiling.*

(03) *Continue raising your arms until they are straight up, with the palms facing each other above your head. Concentrate your attention* *on an area on the wall opposite you at eye level, so your head remains centred.*

While in this position, keep your breathing slow, deep, and regular. Imagine that your feet have become at one with the floor and that you are utterly immovable.

Reverse the movements to bring yourself back to the starting position.

The lunchtime break

The rule is that, unless there is an exceptionally good reason, the lunchtime break is reserved for yourself. Perhaps lunch for you is a plate of nourishing food (see pp. 24–31) followed by a chapter of your book. Maybe it is an easy jog followed by a healthy smoothie (see p. 28). It might even be some form of organized exercise class (see pp. 32–7). Or you might use part of your break for an invigorating meditation (see p. 100). What you must not do is increase stress levels further by working through lunch, snatching mouthfuls of sandwich washed down with coffee (see p. 21).

FOOD IS MORE THAN FUEL
Integrate your lunchtime eating and drinking into a complete strategy for minimizing the stress in your life. For example, are you looking for a snack? Then

HEALTHY EATING
What you eat at lunchtime can help heal the effects of a stressful morning as well as fortify you for a busy afternoon. The fibre and carbohydrates in grains, such as rice, are essential for a healthy, stress-healing diet. And the vitamins, minerals, flavonoids, proteins, and fibre in raw or lightly cooked vegetables are part of what you need for a balanced nutritional intake.

almonds are full of monounsaturated fats, which help to lower cholesterol levels in the body. In addition, they are an effective remedy for easing many stress-related stomach complaints. As a flavouring in food, lemon balm works on the part of the brain that deals with mood and temperament, easing the effects of anxiety and depression. You can also use lemon balm as a calming herbal tea, lowering blood pressure and reducing nervous palpitations. Beetroot, too, helps to regulate blood pressure, and it is an ideal vegetable to add to salads if you suffer from excessive stomach acidity and other nervous digestive complaints, such as heartburn. Well known for treating digestive-tract problems, ginger is also suitable whenever you need relief from a nervous headache or migraine. And basil is a general tonic, helping to sharpen your concentration and memory as well as lessening depression and anxiety.

LUNCHTIME ACTIVITIES
Keep a change of clothes at work and go for a lunchtime jog. Having a running partner might help your motivation on those days when you are low and don't feel like going out.

A lunchtime yoga class, or any other form of exercise regime, can help to bring about feelings of peace and calm by burning off the stress-inducing hormones in your bloodstream. Exercise classes are commonly found in health clubs, community halls, medical health centres, and so on.

TENSION-RELIEVING MEDITATION

By concentrating your entire attention on a particular object, such as a crystal, candle, religious icon, or flower, you can let the tension and anxiety flow from your body.

- *Sit comfortably in a quiet space and spend a few minutes concentrating on your chosen object. Allow nothing to distract you as the image of the object imprints itself on your mind. Notice its colours, its textures, the play of light and shade over its surface. Let the object's image push all other thoughts, worries, concerns out of your mind.*

- *Once every detail of the object is firmly fixed in your mind, cup your hands over your eyes to exclude all light. Don't allow the absence of vision to mar the perfect image you have of the object.*

- *Feel all the muscles in your body start to relax as a warming glow emanates from the object. See the aura of light expand and expand, encompassing your entire body.*

- *Enjoy the safe, warm, comfortable feeling for about 10 minutes before coming back to your surroundings.*

CHI KUNG

This system of exercise, also spelled qi gong, originated in China. The exercises concentrate on marshalling the body's life-force energies (qi) into a powerful mind–body healing system. By stimulating blood flow around the body and balancing the flow of energy, the routine shown here, known as the "three taps", can help you to let go of the tensions and anxieties that have built up during your morning's work.

01  **02**  **03**

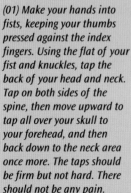

(01) Make your hands into fists, keeping your thumbs pressed against the index fingers. Using the flat of your fist and knuckles, tap the back of your head and neck. Tap on both sides of the spine, then move upward to tap all over your skull to your forehead, and then back down to the neck area once more. The taps should be firm but not hard. There should not be any pain.

(02) Gently tap the kidney areas using the back of your fist. Tap the right kidney and then the left kidney, and tap from the top of the kidney to the bottom. There is no set time for this, but try 1–2 minutes for each kidney.

(03) Using your middle knuckles, tap the middle of your chest for approximately 2 minutes. Tap in a series of threes, with the first tap being heavier than the other two – almost like tapping out the rhythm of a heartbeat.

This sequence of taps is very stimulating and you will be surprised how invigorated and stress free you feel afterward.

Stress-free working at home

Some estimates put the number of people who will be working from home within the next 10 years as high as one in three. Take away the daily commute, those hours not spent in stalled, rush-hour traffic or on crowded buses or trains; think about all the time saved by avoiding idle office gossip and meaningless workplace rituals, and working at home sounds like heaven. Or does it?

DIVISION OF SPACE
One of the loudest signals that comes through from people who have made the change is that, for the transition to be successful, you need a clear distinction between work space and office space, between work time and home time. It is difficult to lay down rules as we are all so different, but the habit of "going to work" is deeply ingrained in many of us. So, having a

FRAGRANT SOLUTIONS
A big plus of working from home is you can fragrance your space as you please. In a special oil burner, add 3 drops lavender essential oil and 2 of rose to 20ml (1 tablespoon) of carrier oil for anxiety; to aid memory, use 4 drops rosemary and 1 each of laurel and peppermint; to boost feelings of low morale, add 2 drops each of thyme, pine, and cedarwood oil.

TAKE STOCK

This reiki exercise (right) is called Stop! It gives you the space you need to take stock of the physical behaviour and mental and emotional patterns that may be responsible for those niggly aches and pains and feelings of depression or being unable to cope.

- *At any point during the day, no matter what you are doing when the thought occurs to you, STOP your activities. Just freeze in position and note your posture – slouched, hunched, awkwardly held, and so on. Note, too, what you were thinking about when you froze. Were you fully engaged in what you were doing? Were you wishing you were somewhere else? Take note of your feelings about your situation at that precise moment. Spend between 30 and 60 seconds taking stock in this fashion.*

- *Resume your normal activities.*

REASONS IN FAVOUR

■ *Zero commuting time and no commuting expenses.*

■ *You can slot domestic chores into the working day and so free-up time on weekends.*

■ *You can wear clothes you feel most comfortable in.*

■ *You can make yourself healthy drinks whenever you wish and eat whatever you feel like at lunchtime.*

■ *There are no office politics to distract you.*

■ *You can take short breaks whenever it suits you, and read a chapter of a book or listen to music when you need a change of pace.*

■ *You can control the lighting, heating, and ventilation levels so you are optimally comfortable.*

■ *As well as working you can also feel more a part of the local community.*

■ *You can tailor your working hours to suit your family requirements.*

separate room in the home (or a well-built summer house in the garden or converted space in the attic), which is the office you "go" to every morning, is an enormous help. It is also somewhere you can close off at the end of the working day when it's time to turn your attention to your family or personal life.

Stress levels are bound to rise with the inevitable resentment that comes from not drawing a clear distinction between these two parts of your life. If one area of your home must do double duty as domestic and work space, then screen off the computer or filing cabinet at the end of the day so it is not constantly competing for your attention.

THE RIGHT PERSONALITY
The next most important consideration to take into account before deciding on a home-working lifestyle is whether you are a "people person" or not. Some of us find it difficult to find the necessary motivation unless we are part of a team or are able to bounce ideas off colleagues and get their immediate feedback. If this sounds like you, then the isolation of home-working might be a source of anxiety in itself. Webcams and teleconferencing facilities mean, of course, that while at home you can speak to any number of colleagues simultaneously and even make eye contact – if, of course, your job makes this approach suitable.

FAMILY SUPPORT
Finally, unless you live alone, then the decision to turn part of your home into a place of work needs to be a joint one. You need to have the support of your family to make a success of the transition.

REASONS AGAINST
- *It can be difficult to haul yourself out of bed in the mornings without having a boss to check on your time-keeping.*

- *More self-discipline is needed to stop you doing the housework, shopping, gardening, or watching daytime television when you really need to be working.*

- *It can be expensive to set up a room as a home office. Running costs – such as telephone, heating, air conditioning, equipment, insurances, and so on – may be high.*

- *You might miss the buzz of a busy workplace.*

- *You might feel you are being sidelined at work because you are not there to fight your corner.*

- *You may become bored and feel lonely without your work colleagues.*

- *You may be the type of person who needs feedback from colleagues.*

Coping with redundancy

Redundancy, if it happens to you, can have a range of devastating effects. Losing your job not only means losing your source of income, your sense of self-worth is also intimately involved. This is so even if you know that you are in no way responsible for what has happened to you. Other emotions you are likely to experience, especially in the initial stages, are fear, rejection, and despair. People also commonly report experiencing a sense of shame and failure, desperate feelings that are only intensified when you need to tell family and friends.

Once the shock has modified somewhat, the overwhelming emotion is anger. "Why me? I gave my best years to that company. How can they ruin my life like this? It's like I don't matter."

The best way to turn this situation around is to manage the change the redundancy has wrought – rather than regarding the event as the end of your productive life, see it, instead, as an opportunity to move on and improve your circumstances. Rather than trying to find an equivalent job in a similar company, you may, for example, decide that this is the perfect opportunity to change direction completely, to find a different path. Whichever route you decide to go, consider the following:

■ Make sure you receive everything you are entitled to as part of your redundancy package. If your company has a human resources (personnel) department, check your legal entitlement and ask if management will pay for financial planning advice for you or provide

BE POSITIVE ABOUT CHANGE

Stress will be less of an issue for you as well as your family if you adopt a positive approach to your situation. To achieve this, it helps to understand the phases you need to pass through.

In the first phase it's crucial to accept the inevitability of change. Look for soul-mates you can confide in and who will help and encourage you to be outgoing and embrace change.

In the second phase you need to put into action your plans for the future. Marshal your mental resources, which should be robust after the efforts you put into the first phase, sort out your financial affairs, and put into effect your job-hunting/ skills-updating strategies.

In the final phase you need to assess whether or not the changes you have made in your life, and the new attitudes you have adopted, are now genuinely a part of the "new you". If you are simply going through the motions, and thus papering over the problems, stress and anxiety will continue to be issues for you.

help in retraining or careers advice as part of your severance. If you are unhappy with the response you get, contact your union, if relevant, a legal advisor, or the citizens' advice bureau to see where you stand.

- Take a reality check. Your sole, or primary, source of income is gone, hopefully only temporarily. Even so, the way to minimize the stress of the situation is to make best use of the financial resources you have available. List every outgoing: mortgage, credit cards, utilities, car payments, food, entertainment, school fees, clothes, magazines and newspapers, and so on. Decide which of these you can do without and cut them out of your budget. Next, prioritize your outgoings to ensure you have sufficient funds for the really crucial things, such as the mortgage. If you run a car, you may decide it is an unnecessary expense in your changed circumstances. However, if public transport is unreliable or unavailable, or owning a car is crucial to your job-seeking plans, it moves far higher up the list of priorities. Contact your mortgage provider and credit card issuers, explain your new situation, and try to negotiate a temporary payments moratorium or reduced payments for a time. It is better to be upfront with your creditors rather than fall behind with payments. Remember, your situation is not unique.

- Revise your curriculum vitae (résumé), trawl through newspapers or magazines/journals relevant to your occupation, and look at likely websites to find potential employers. Rather than send out the same

USE YOUR TIME, AND YOUR MIND

Having been made redundant, you are likely to have more free time on your hands than you have been used to. Resist the temptation to become obsessed with housework, unnecessary do-it-yourself projects, or watching the afternoon soaps. Think instead of how you can best use your time, and your mind – perhaps through some form of voluntary work.

You may, for example, feel like spending your time doing voluntary work at your local hospital, library, or school. If you have particular skills – computer expertise, say – you might want to volunteer at a youth centre, passing on your knowledge to young people.

The advantage of this is it will bring you out of your shell, it will help you keep your social skills finely honed, you will make new contacts, you will be able to feel positive about yourself, and you will not feel bored or useless.

curriculum vitae (résumé) to everybody, tailor its contents to emphasize the areas of your experience that seem most relevant and downplay the others.

■ Revise your job opportunities. Look at the possibility of going back to college or taking on a training course to update your skills-base. You might also want to think about retraining for a completely new career – perhaps your hobby of gardening, for example, could be transformed into a career in landscaping via a short bridging course.

■ Take care of yourself. Redundancy is bound to be a stressful time and your anxiety levels could become high. The more you bottle up your fears and anxieties, the worse they are likely to become. Although difficult, let your feelings out to close family and good friends and resist the temptation to withdraw from normal social and family life. Talking your options through with another person is likely to help clarify your situation and reveal the choices you do have. If you simply can't confide in friends or family for any reason, seek professional help from a trained counsellor. Your family doctor is the best starting point if you don't have a personal recommendation to go by.

■ Claim all your benefits. With a reduced family income, you may be entitled to allowances in addition to basic unemployment benefits, such as a rebate on your council tax or help with retraining costs.

CHAPTER FIVE

Social and family life

Stress permeates every aspect of your life. It simply cannot be conveniently compartmentalized. So if you are stressed at work, then for certain you will be bringing the problem back into your home, to the detriment of your social and family life.

Many of the precautions that you take at work to minimize the effects that stress and anxiety place on you and your performance (see pp. 76–109) have direct parallels in the home. Just as you need to organize your desk and stress-proof your working space, for example, in the home you need to pay attention to the stress-inducing effects of domestic clutter, as well as how the right sounds, appropriate colours, and full-spectrum lighting can all help you to let go and relax. And just as meditation and exercise can dispel anxiety and tension at work, so, too, can they do the same when you come to unwind and enjoy your social and family life at home.

We all at some time or another have trouble getting the work–life balance right. Work schedules can become so pressurized and timing so crucial that they take over and push everything else in life to one side. And while you might expect sympathy and understanding from family and friends, at least for a while, you should not be that surprised when, at some point, your nearest and dearest become tired of playing the supporting act to an adrenaline-addicted workaholic.

And when it comes to your love life, stress can be a real passion killer. Sexual dysfunction among people affected by chronic stress is surprisingly high, but with the right ambience, a little good food and wine followed by a sensual massage, you may be retiring to the bedroom earlier than expected.

Stress-proofing your home

Home is your haven, the place where you feel safe, where you can pull up the drawbridge and fend off the assaults of the outside world. It is somewhere you can relax and unwind and allow the stresses of the day to fall away. But if it is not, perhaps you need to do something about it.

CLUTTER AND STRESS

The connection between clutter and stress is clear. Get out of bed in the morning and trip over your shoes lying half hidden under the discarded bedspread. Throw on your clothes and limp to the kitchen, picking your way down a hallway littered with children's toys and books to find the usual cascade of unsorted newspapers, odd articles of clothing, countertops overflowing with letters, bills, and assorted junk mail, sticky notes, broken fridge magnets, a vase of near-dead flowers, and photocopies of articles yet to be read – not to mention last night's washing-up. Spend an obligatory ten minutes looking for the one page of the work you were doing last night that you really do need with you this morning and then another five minutes playing hunt the car keys. How are your stress levels doing?

Feng shui

According to the practice of feng shui, it is vital to keep your home clutter-free if you are not to cause blockages in the flow of *chi* (or vital energy) in it. Hallways and stairways, for example, are crucial connecting areas and should be kept clear of

A PLACE FOR EVERYTHING
The old saying goes: A place for everything, and everything in its place. Feng shui recommends that clutter-attracting surfaces, such as tables, should be cleared periodically of everything that should be kept somewhere else. This prevents chi becoming stale and harmful. So get rid of hairbrushes, half-finished glasses of juice, your child's toy tractor, computer disks, and so on, and confine odds and ends, such as your car keys, to a small dish so you always know where they are.

obstructions at all times, otherwise the flow of chi around your home will suffer. Likewise in the kitchen – a build-up of clutter here can be dangerous, not only for the obvious reason that hot surfaces and sharp implements can be potentially lethal, but also because clutter can cause health-afflicting energy to enter into the food you and your family consume.

It is in the bedroom, however, that you need to pay particular attention to order and tidiness if you want that space to remain special, your inner sanctum (see right). Taking away the clutter in this room strips the confusion from your mind, encouraging spiritual calm and restful, healing sleep.

DECLUTTER THE BEDROOM

Include only your favourite things in this room and put away all the paraphernalia of normal life in drawers and wardrobes. A mirror reflecting the bed is considered bad feng shui, as it can place a strain on your relationship. Natural light is very important, so keep windows as clear of obstructions as possible.

STRESS-PROOFING TOOLS

The practice of feng shui offers you a range of tools to help stress-proof your home. Many of these tools are intended to ease the flow of chi energy around your house or apartment, while others act as a calming aid to concentration. Blocked or stale energy is often a reflection of your lifestyle and your state of mind. So feng shui is more effective when you undertake a reform of all aspects of your life, including exercise, diet, and meditation – unblock your body's internal channels and you will help to release the mind.

CANDLES

Using a lighted candle as a focus point can be a great help as an aid to concentration. Focus your mind on the flame and allow it to push all other thoughts out of your consciousness. As the light fills your thoughts, feel the tension and stress fall away.

INCENSE

Many religions and cultures around the world use incense as a way to purify the atmosphere and still the mind.

SINGING BOWL

A home where malevolent energy, or sickness chi, is present generates the stress of ill health, for you or your family members. The resonant note of a well-made singing bowl will dispel this chi, purifying the air and producing an atmosphere in which you can achieve your full stress-management potential.

BELLS

Use the clear sound of a bell to revitalize and invigorate yourself.

WIND CHIMES

Wherever there is negative chi in your home, you will find it difficult to dispel the gloomy thoughts that accompany stress and anxiety. So, to prevent this form of chi entering your home, hang a metal-rod wind chime at the entrance, outside the door where it will catch the slightest breeze. Even if you are sceptical about the technique, try it out for a few weeks and see if your mood lightens.

SMUDGE STICKS

Bundles of herbs, called smudge sticks, can be burned as part of a purification ritual to cleanse a person or place of negative chi or evil influences. Some people find "smudging" especially beneficial when they have been feeling stressed, anxious, depressed, angry, or resentful.

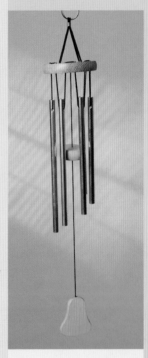

COLOUR AND LIGHT

Colour has a large part to play in stress-proofing your home. What we see as colour is, in fact, the reflection or transmission of selective parts of the electro-magnetic spectrum. This encompasses not only the narrow band of visible light, but also radio waves, infrared, ultraviolet, and X-rays.

For the bedroom you want to produce a welcoming, soft, and relaxing colour scheme, an effect that favours the warm pinks and gentle oranges – both hues from the red end of the visible spectrum. Other colours suitable for a stress-free bedroom include the off-white tints, ranging from eggshell through to beige. The more fully saturated reds and oranges are probably too powerful for this area of the home.

In the kitchen, use colours such as yellows or something from the earth range of hues – chestnut, brown, dark beige, or ochre, for example. In your living room, you could try a very pale shade of blue, but bear in mind that you need to treat this colour with a degree of respect, as it is known to encourage introspection (characterized by the expression "feeling blue"). It can also make a room seem cold. A better colour might be one of the softer shades of green, a hue that is also suitable for the bedroom or a bathroom.

The modern trend toward neutral colour in the home means there are a lot of white walls out there. Brilliant white, especially large areas of it, is often too stark for a stress-free atmosphere, so it is better to opt for one of the warm, off-white shades for the bedroom and other social areas of the home, and one of the cooler shades of off-white for bathrooms, utility rooms, and other practical areas of the house.

MEDITATION ZONE
A warm, off-white tint is the most suitable shade for a meditation area in your home, and candle flames are a useful aid to meditation (see p. 115). But to assist you in "letting go" of your physical surroundings, clear away all the extraneous clutter that could act as a distraction. What is useful, however, is a cushion to sit on and, close by, a shawl in case you get cold.

Warning: If you are using lighted candles, especially when meditating, always ensure that the flames are well away from anything flammable and that they cannot topple over and start a fire.

ELECTROMAGNETIC FIELDS (EMFs)

Being aware of the detrimental effects of EMFs is as important in the home as it is in the office (see p. 80). To lessen the likelihood of complaints such as stress-induced headaches, migraines, and disturbed sleep, disconnect all electrical devices when they are not in use. In the bedroom, for example, unplug the TV before going to sleep, and rather than having an electric clock, use a traditional clockwork type instead.

Although these precautions will help, EMFs are also associated with the wiring in the walls or under the floorboards. In most rooms there is little you can do about this, but in one room at least – your bedroom, say – you might consider taking out all electrical wiring.

FULL-SPECTRUM LIGHTING

The suspicion that lighting has an effect on health was first confirmed during experiments on mice. Living under fluorescent lighting, which is deficient in some frequencies in full-spectrum daylight, it was noted that they lived for less than half the time of mice kept in natural light.

In the winter months especially, when daylight levels are often low, we can be reliant on domestic lighting much of the time. Some people, however, are particularly sensitive to the missing frequencies in this lighting and fall victim to Seasonal Affective Disorder, or SAD. Symptoms include depression, tension, lack of libido, inability to cope with normal stress, cravings for carbohydrates, and increased premenstrual tension.

Full-spectrum artificial lighting is now readily available, though severe instances of SAD may require exposure to high-intensity "daylight" lightboxes.

CRYSTALS

In addition to being decorative items in your home, crystals, such as the rose quartz shown opposite, possess special powers. Thought to have excellent healing and protecting properties, extending to anybody living in your home, this gemstone can also help to reinforce emotional wellbeing when you are feeling vulnerable. Also known as roselle, pale pink rose quartz is principally associated with feelings of friendship and boosting self-confidence.

The work–life balance

Your mantra should be: I work to live, not live to work. For the one in six full-time employees in the UK working in excess of 60 hours a week, however, this ideal remains, sadly, merely an aspiration. And add to this an average daily commute of about one hour or more each way, and the weekly total creeps up to a staggering 80+ hours.

The link between working long hours and stress is well documented. Surveys show that nearly a third of employees with high stress levels work more than 10 hours longer per week than their contractual hours. Even more worrying, 70 per cent of these highly stressed individuals are locked into rigid work practices that do not allow them any flexibility over their hours of employment.

The results are clear: employers suffer through increased absentee rates and the poor efficiency of their staff when they are at work, while employees pay the price of a severely devalued quality of life as they constantly juggle the demands of home and work, squeezing more and more into the day.

Work, however, must not always be cast in the role of villain. For many people, work is their sole or primary creative outlet; it can broaden our outlook and provide us with the means of discovering more of the world we live in. Just as too much work causes a work–life imbalance, so, too, does too little. In addition, the workplace may be where we interact with most of our friends or the place where we make most of our new social contacts.

STRIKE THE RIGHT BALANCE

- *Leave for work in plenty of time to ensure you are not late. That way, you will have one less excuse for staying after hours.*

- *If you are regularly asked to work late or at weekends, learn to say "No".*

- *Make social commitments well in advance so you can organize your work to accommodate them.*

- *Leave your work at the workplace. Don't bring paperwork or projects home with you. Reserve your home time for your partner and family.*

- *Don't let stress make you withdraw into yourself. Keep talking to your partner about any fears or worries you may be experiencing.*

Family events

We are accustomed to think of stress resulting from negative occurrences – work pressures, inadequate housing, relationship problems, money worries, traffic jams, constant noise, and so on – so it is interesting to note that many stress-inducing life events are, in fact, "happy occasions". For example, according to the Holmes-Rahe scale (see pp. 18–19), a family vacation and celebrating Christmas rate as numbers 39 and 40 on the list of most stressful life events, while a wedding rates much higher up the list, coming in at number 7. Even more revealing is that work-related events make up only three of the top 20 most stressful life events.

STRESS BY-PASS
With a major family event looming, the more preplanning you can do, the less opportunity there will be for things to get on top of you. Consider the following tips for a stress-free wedding:

■ Try positive, or targeted, visualization techniques, in which you envisage every step of the wedding preparations going with textbook precision (see pp. 42–3 and 48). Use as an image with the visualization the happy faces of your family and friends enjoying themselves at the event.

■ It is the last-minute panics that make events such as weddings difficult to deal with. Make a detailed checklist and then give yourself more than enough time to achieve each point.

- Don't be over-ambitious. Your stress levels will only increase if you try to make the event more elaborate than you can reasonably achieve, or more costly than you can reasonably afford.

- Wherever you can, delegate. Passing over the responsibility of some of the arrangements to others you trust will make the event more enjoyable for you and will help to cement the bonds of friendship.

- Listen to suggestions about how the wedding day can best be celebrated from those most intimately involved in the event. That way, stress levels will be generally lowered.

A HAPPY OCCASION?
We all expect a family wedding to be a happy occasion. However, getting married rates more highly in terms of stress than getting fired from work, according to the Holmes-Rahe scale.

Unwinding at home

Your home time is a precious commodity. It is when you can devote your time and energy to pleasing yourself and caring for your friends and family. But how often can you honestly say that you spent the entire evening at home and never once let your mind wander back to the events of the working day?

The best way to ensure that you do not continue stressing about work once you are at home is to develop a set pattern – a ritual if you like – that tells you at a very fundamental level that the working day is over and done with. You will need to find the elements of the ritual that best suit you (such as those suggested right), but as a first step, try shedding your stress along with your clothes as you step into a relaxing hot bath or shower. Add calming lavender aromatherapy essential oil to your bath water or burn lavender oil in the bathroom so that it is taken up with the steam from your shower. If you prefer, there are many gentle exercise routines ideal for unwinding after work, such as the yoga stretches given on the following pages.

It is tempting and all too easy to become reliant on chemical fixes to relieve the symptoms of stress. Alcohol, for example, can have a sedative effect in the short term, although it is likely to disrupt your sleep patterns if consumed in excess or taken during the evening in conjunction with the other common chemical stimulant, caffeine (see pp. 20–1). It is better to develop a taste for fruit juices, herbal teas (there are many caffeine-free types to choose from), or plain mineral water (see pp. 24–9).

FORMULA FOR SUCCESS
Follow these points for a relaxing evening at home:

- *Change into clothes you feel really relaxed in. If you are concerned about your belly, for example, stop sucking it in and wear a baggy top that covers it up.*

- *Fill your home with the calming, soothing aroma of your favourite incense.*

- *Turn the lights down low and use candles for accent lighting.*

- *Listen to music you particularly enjoy. If you can play an instrument, then make time for a little relaxing practice.*

- *Stroking a pet, such as a cat or a dog, is proven to be good for your health by lowering blood pressure. And the stress-relieving benefits of a well-cared-for tank of fish is testified to by their near-universal presence in dentists' waiting rooms.*

EASY YOGA STRETCHES

Stress, and the tension it sets up in your body, is most commonly felt in the neck and shoulder region. A few minutes spent on these basic yoga stretching exercises as part of your unwinding routine will pay enormous dividends (see also pp. 128–9).

The model in these photographs is shown sitting in the half-lotus. This position is not essential, however, so if you have any problems with it, sitting cross-legged is fine – just keep your back as straight as possible throughout. The more often you practise these exercises, the more flexible your body will become, but never push yourself further than is comfortable, especially in the beginning.

VERTICAL STRETCH

(01) Sit in the half-lotus, if you can. If not, sit cross-legged with a straight back and head looking directly forward. Roll your shoulders slowly to loosen them up.

(02) Slowly start to lift both arms simultaneously until your palms meet above your head. Stay in this position for 5 seconds, holding your breath. Exhaling, lower your arms to the start position. Repeat 3 times.

01

02

01

03

HORIZONTAL STRETCHES

(01) Sitting in the half-lotus position or cross-legged, stretch your arms forward, palms touching, and thumbs interlocked. Keep your arms at shoulder height. Lower your head until your chin presses against your chest. Make sure to keep your back straight. Breathe normally in this position for 5 seconds.

(02) As you inhale, throw your hands apart and start to move your arms backward as far as they will go. As you do this look upward. Hold your breath in this position for 5 seconds. You will definitely feel a stretch in your shoulders and neck, but it is important to go only as far as your body comfortably allows. You will find that gradually you can stretch further and further back.

(03) After 5 seconds, start to move your arms forward as you exhale, bringing your arms back to the position in step 01. Bring your head down again until you feel your chin pressing against your chest. Repeat 2 times.

DIAGONAL STRETCHES

(01) Sitting in the half-lotus position, or comfortably cross-legged if you prefer, with a straight back, stretch your arms out to the sides. Keep your arms at shoulder height with your palms facing the floor.

(02) Inhaling, twist your body as far as you can to the left without straining. At the same time, turn your head back to look at your left hand. Keep your hands at shoulder height. Stay in this position for 5 seconds, holding your breath.

(03) Exhaling, now twist your body to the right and turn your head back to look at your right hand. Stay in this position for 5 seconds, holding your breath. Repeat this 2 times on each side.

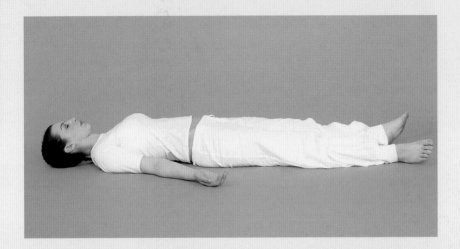

THE CORPSE POSE

Another excellent exercise for relieving stress when you arrive home from work is known as the corpse position, or *shavasana*. The relaxation it produces makes it an excellent pose to adopt between exercises, as it allows your muscles to relax and aids circulation.

Find a quiet space where you have plenty of room, and lie comfortably on your back. Let your arms fall a little away from your body with palms facing upward and your fingers in a naturally relaxed curl. Keep your legs slightly apart and allow your feet to splay outward naturally. Breathe slowly and deeply, matching the length of your inhalations and exhalations. As you lie there breathing in a calm, relaxed fashion, feel all the tensions of your day seeping out of your body into the floor. Concentrate on each part of your body in turn, loosening all the tension you discover.

THE BENEFITS TO YOU

The corpse pose brings a range of benefits. Not only is it deeply relaxing and helps to stimulate blood circulation, but it also sharpens your concentration as you tackle the tension in each part of your body in turn. As a result, feelings of nervousness, fatigue, indigestion, and breathlessness can be alleviated after 10–15 minutes. If you are adopting the corpse pose as a link between different exercises, hold the position for about 3 minutes only.

De-stressing your love life

Feeling overworked and under pressure a lot of the time? Up against impossible deadlines at work and feeling unable to cope more often than you used to? Experiencing frequent headaches and chronic discomfort in the neck and shoulders? Haven't had a good night's sleep for what seems like weeks? If so, then it is not all that surprising that your romantic life is suffering.

And research suggests that most of these problems, leading to sexual dysfunction in between a third and a half of men and women, are the result of self-imposed pressures – those you place on yourself through lifestyle choices such as where you live, commuting, diet, occupation, alcohol consumption, indebtedness, and so on. Although "Let's put it in the diary" may sound a bit like a joke, perhaps it is not so silly. After all, it is not really silly that you and your partner should plan in advance for a romantic evening at home together. Good food, a little wine, soft lighting, music, the delicate scents of your favourite essential oils. Who knows what it might lead to?

FOOD FOR LOVE
A romantic meal for two should be tempting and delicious, simple to prepare yet subtly complex in flavour and texture, and, most important of all, it should be substantial enough to take the edge off your hunger without being too heavy. Nothing is more likely to take the romantic edge off the evening than falling into a contented stupor as your body wrestles with the task of digestion.

A few suggestions for light, temptingly tasty romantic meals that are easy to prepare include:

- Smoked salmon cooked in crème fraîche, flavoured with chives and lemon.

- Fresh mussels cooked in a spicy Tunisian sauce, flavoured with coriander and served with crusty bread.

- A vegetarian white bean soup, flavoured with a hint of garlic, thyme, leeks, and a little potato.

TAKE TIME TO TALK
Keep the lines of communication open. Make sure each of you is completely honest and tells the other person your feelings, your fears, your hopes, and your dreams. Touch is a crucial part of good communication, as is proper eye contact.

SENSUAL MASSAGE

Once you have eaten a light meal, perhaps accompanied by a little wine, turn the lights down low, or light some candles, put some relaxing music on quietly in the background, and learn once more the pleasure of being in your partner's arms. If you like, the next step in de-stressing your love life could be a wonderful sensual massage. It is a good idea to cut your nails short before giving a massage, as long nails can be painful.

Mix a few drops of massage oil into slightly warmed carrier oil (see right). Pour some of the oil into your cupped hand and then rub both hands together to distribute the oil. With your partner lying on a bed or a massage mat on the floor, begin massaging the shoulders and upper back using long, slow, exploring strokes. Work on both sides of the spine, moving down the back. Note your partner's responses to your contact and concentrate on the areas that give most pleasure. From the back, move onto the arms, massaging right down to the fingers. Then move to the hips, buttocks, thighs, calves, and feet, using more oil as necessary to keep your hands well lubricated.

Knead the fleshy areas, rolling the skin between your fingers, using as much pressure as your partner enjoys. If you are unsure, ask for feedback so you know how to give maximum pleasure. Finish off the massage with light, sweeping movements of your hands, allowing your fingers to glide tantalizingly all over the body.

With a soft, clean towel wipe off any excess oil. Then swap places so that you, too, can enjoy the pleasure of a sensual massage.

MASSAGE OILS
Depending on your preference, you can use bergamot, camomile, lavender, marjoram, melissa, or rosemary aromatherapy essential oils, among others. Carrier oils include apricot, avocado, coconut, grapeseed, and sweet almond.

For a full-body massage, you will need about 5–6 tablespoons of carrier oil, into which you should mix about 5–7 drops of the essential oil.

CAUTIONS
- *Do not massage a woman in the first trimester of pregnancy.*
- *Avoid massaging any areas of broken skin or where there is bruising, swelling, or inflammation.*

PLEASURE PALACE

Now that you have wined and dined (see pp. 130–1), pleasured each other by giving and receiving a sensual massage (see pp. 132–3), this is the moment to initiate the most intimate act. Or is it?

If your evening has gone well, both of you should be feeling secure and safe enough with each other to make love only if that is what you both desire. After all, nothing is more likely to generate stress and feelings of anxiety than believing that the preceding meal and the massage somehow oblige you to perform sexually, even if your libido is out of synch with that of your partner.

Sex can be a deep and tender form of communication, one that is made all the more meaningful when you and your partner are free from any inhibitions and are completely relaxed in each other's company. Removing the barriers that get in the way of good sex, however, normally means both of you talking through your wants and needs. Don't assume that by a process of osmosis, or something similar, the other person will somehow realize what your secrets are, those desires that perhaps you have not even fully admitted to yourself. If you don't talk about sex, there is room for doubt and misunderstanding to creep into the relationship – both in and out of bed.

If vocalizing your intimate secrets is a step too far, then try using touch as a substitute form of communication. Spontaneous acts of hugging, kissing, and hand-holding can establish the type of trust that breaks down barriers and establishes intimacy.

The principal therapies

Their are many therapies with a proven track record in relieving the symptoms of stress and anxiety. Some of the more important ones used in this book are briefly defined here.

AROMATHERAPY

The term "aromatherapy" was first devised by Frenchman Henri Maurice Gattefosse in 1928 to describe a new field of study he was investigating – the use of aromatic plant oils to promote healing. His interest began when he thrust his hand into a container of lavender oil after burning it in a laboratory accident. His hand apparently healed far quicker than expected and there was very little scarring.

This was not an entirely new discovery. Records exist that Babylonians used the medicinal qualities of aromatic plant oils more than 7,000 years ago. Likewise, many cultures down the centuries have used plant oils for healing, though Gattefosse's real contribution is the scientific documentation of the different plant oils and their beneficial qualities.

CHI KUNG

Also commonly known as qi gong, chi kung is becoming an increasingly popular type of healing and exercise technique. Its practice essentially involves a system of breathing control that cultivates *chi*, or energy, and transmits it to all the body's vital organs.

Known in ancient China as "the method to repel illness and prolong life", today it is mainly taught as a health-maintenance system, and various forms of chi kung are widely taught in conjunction with Chinese martial arts.

COLOUR HEALING

The use of colour to influence our mental and physical wellbeing has been part of cultural practice in many different civilizations for millennia, including Egyptian, Greek, Chinese, Tibetan, Indian, and Mayan. In Europe, however, much of this ancient wisdom was lost during the Dark Ages, appearing once more only when the likes of Newton and Goethe began to revise interest in the power of light and colour from the eighteenth century.

Used as an adjunct to conventional medicine and other complementary therapies, colour healing can, with knowledge and understanding, help the body to repair a range of physical ailments. These include headaches and poor attention, as well as disorders requiring a rebalancing of the body's energies. In addition, colour healing has a good record in treating stress-related disorders, including depression and the SAD syndrome.

CRYSTAL HEALING

Crystal healing works on the principle that each type of crystal has the ability to retain and focus electromagnetic energy. Crystals can be naturally occurring or created artificially, though those that come from deep within the Earth, where they have been shaped over millennia, have greater potency.

FENG SHUI

Literally translated as "wind and water", feng shui is the 3,000-year-old Chinese art of placement. It is based on a belief in the importance of the movement of *chi*, or energy, through our surroundings. Traditional feng shui concerns itself with the layout of cities, towns, and individual buildings, and teaches that we should seek the places where *chi* forms or collects if we want to live happy and successful lives.

By following the patterns of nature, practitioners advise on how to place everything, from the smallest ornament in your home or workplace to the position and orientation of an entire building within its site, for optimum luck. Feng shui also shows us how to control the flow of *chi* to bring about good luck in all our dealings in the material world as well as in our emotional relationships.

MASSAGE

Massage is manipulation of the body's soft tissue and is designed to: bring about general health benefits, such as relieving insomnia or improving relaxation; have specific physical benefits, such as the relief of aches and pains or improving muscle tone after injury; or as an intimate form of physical communication, as in sensual massage.

Too much stress in our lives produces muscular tension and bad posture. This muscular "dis-ease" restricts the flow of blood around the body, starving the muscles and organs of crucial oxygen. Another consequence of this muscular tension is that some of the toxins that would normally be removed by a healthy flow of blood are left behind to build up in the body. Prolonged muscular stress can also affect the skeleton itself, making existing problems worse and creating new ones.

MEDITATION

Used for thousands of years, especially by Eastern civilizations, meditation is a safe and simple way to balance your physical, emotional, and mental states of being. Meditation usually entails entering a state of extreme relaxation and concentration by focusing your mind on a single point of reference – such as the chanting of a "mantra", for example. This helps to put your body in a state of rest and frees you from distracting superficial thoughts.

Meditation is now used by many non-religious practitioners, although it also forms part of several major religions. Known to reduce levels of stress hormone in the body, meditation is becoming increasingly popular as a method of general stress relief. It is also beneficial for improving the body's self-healing abilities and strengthening resistance to disease and illness.

NEURO-LINGUISTIC PROGRAMMING

Known commonly by the acronym NLP, this therapy represents a technique for bringing about positive changes in behaviour. Whether you have very specific goals you wish to achieve or, alternatively, you are looking simply to widen your range of life skills, NLP may be suitable.

There are three main components to NLP. First, the neurological element regulates how your body works; second, the language element governs the way we communicate with other people; and third, the programming component is concerned with the types of models you have of the outside world you interact with.

In essence, NLP holds that the language you use is a reflection of your inner perceptions, and to alter these perceptions, if they are inaccurate, you need to construct new models and new language to describe them.

PILATES

This technique was invented by German-born Joseph H. Pilates (1880–1967). Bearing its inventor's name, pilates concentrates on improving flexibility and increasing strength overall, but without adding body bulk.

More than just exercise, pilates is a series of controlled movements designed to engage both body and mind. The different movements involved are certainly intended to improve your ability to function on a physical level, but the underlying philosophy is that as your body becomes stronger, more supple, more able, then so, too, does your mind. In this way you are able to cope more readily with both the physical and mental challenges of everyday living.

REFLEXOLOGY

The practice of reflexology is based on an ancient Chinese therapy. It involves the manipulation of specific areas principally on the feet, but also of the hands and ears, that correspond to other parts of the body. Applying pressure to these points stimulates body organs and relieves areas of congestion.

REIKI

This is a Japanese form of healing practice in which energy is transferred through the practitioner's hands, which are held above or on the recipient's body. This transference helps to balance the energy in the patient's body, thus improving its innate ability to heal itself.

Because the purpose of reiki is to increase a person's self-healing potential, it can be of benefit to those suffering from a wide variety of problems – whether physical or mental in nature. Reiki has proved successful in the treatment of ailments ranging from stress and migraine to skin disorders and headaches. It has also been effective when used with psychotherapy, for treating people suffering from emotional trauma.

YOGA

Originating in India, and said to be based on the movement of wild animals, the Hindu practice of yoga dates back at least 4,000 years.

The word *yoga* translates as "union" or "yoking", and the practice aims at a spiritual union between the individual and the Supreme Being through a system of physical and mental exercises.

Often taught as a sequence of poses and breath-control exercises, yoga has grown hugely in popularity in the last 25 years and is now widely recognized as a valuable tool in combating many of the effects of stress. Many studies lead to the conclusion that yoga can be beneficial in the treatment of migraine, headaches, insomnia, obesity, anxiety, and menstrual problems – all widely recognized as often having a stress-related component.

The postures, breath exercises, and meditation practices, which are all part of the yoga discipline, have also been shown in studies to lower blood pressure, improve blood flow, and regulate heart rate.

Index

ACKNOWLEDGEMENTS

Gaia Books would like to thank the
following people for their help in
creating this book:

Models
Felicitas Feigl
Kat Neilson
Jake Powley

Hair and make-up
Roishin Donaghy

PICTURE CREDITS

p. 27tl © Octopus Publishing Group
Limited/David Jordan
p. 29fr © Octopus Publishing Group
Limited/William Reavell